# THOSE MEDDLING WOMEN

# Janice Bailey
# THOSE MEDDLING WOMEN

Judson Press ® Valley Forge

THOSE MEDDLING WOMEN

Copyright © 1977
Judson Press, Valley Forge, PA 19481

**Library of Congress Cataloging in Publication Data**

Bailey, Janice.
    Those meddling women.

    Includes bibliographical references.
    1. Women in public life—United States—
Biography.    I. Title.
HQ1412.B34                          920.72'0973                    77-3891
ISBN 0-8170-0757-1

The name JUDSON PRESS is registered as a trademark in the U.S. Patent Office.

Printed in the U.S.A.

## BEFORE HER TIME

She wore the mantle of femininity
Softly, naturally
No time for trappings
Nor for "a woman's place"
But rather for the urgency
Of what she had to do
Discarding outworn labels casually
Like a caterpillar shedding its cocoon
Emerging, beautiful, in fulfillment
Before her time.

*—June Bailey Harlow*

To My Mother

RAE BYERS BAILEY

Who Has Always Been
My Model for Today

A SPECIAL THANK-YOU
To Jean Adams, Inter-Library Loan Librarian,
Wolfsohn Memorial Library, King of Prussia,
Pennsylvania, for her invaluable assistance to the author
in the research necessary for the writing of this book.

# CONTENTS

# PREFACE

Since the beginning of the human race, the world has been plagued by meddling women.

Some women simply do not know how to mind their own business, how to keep out of affairs that do not concern them, nor how to limit their activities to matters that appropriately constitute a "woman's place."

These are the life stories of six of those meddling women.

One meddled in theology in an age when a woman's brain was believed to be too weak to withstand the strain of profound theological thought.

One meddled in government and politics in a time when the workings of government were considered to be the province of men.

Two meddled in abolition and women's rights in a period when the former was considered a cause to be championed by men only and the latter hardly worthy to be classified as a cause at all.

The fifth meddled in freedom of the spirit, roaming the countryside and taking literally the scriptural injunction to take no thought for the morrow.

The sixth meddled in social reform, prying into conditions that were thought to be too horrible for delicate female sensibilities.

None of the six was a paragon of perfection. All were made of human flesh and blood, with human failings and weaknesses. As is characteristic of the human condition, their faults were their virtues exaggerated.

All six had a common base. Each was religiously motivated in

**11**

the life course she chose to follow. Each possessed a personal integrity that was unshakable in the face of criticism or persecution. Each evolved a life-style for herself that was uniquely her own. Each, in espousing a cause that by the standards of the day lay outside the realm of a woman's sphere, was far ahead of her time. Each meddled and through her meddling made the world a better place for all humanity.

Women have long been lost in the footnotes of history. Slowly, but relentlessly, they are beginning to emerge. Their contributions have been significant in the life course of our nation. Their life models have something of value to say to people today.

That is what this book is all about.

Look out! Here come those meddling women!

# 1

# PROPHET IN THE WILDERNESS

## Anne Hutchinson

### (1591-1643)

## Seeker

Anne Marbury was her father's daughter.

When the Reverend Francis Marbury challenged the practices of the Anglican church in England in the late 1500s, he displayed the same high-spirited temperament that was to characterize his eldest daughter's confrontation with the church and civil authorities of the Massachusetts Bay Colony in America some forty-five years later.

As a hot-blooded young Anglican clergyman, Francis Marbury was twice censured and imprisoned for accusing the bishops of ordaining ministers unfit for their calling. Following his second release from prison, he married Bridget Dryden, a young woman of good family. He made his peace with the church and was appointed preacher of Alford parish in Lincolnshire.

But by the time his daughter Anne was born in 1591, the rebellious cleric had again been silenced for criticizing the bishops and lived as a private gentleman for the next fourteen years. Then, in 1605, the church, probably influenced by Marbury's titled relatives, gave him a London parish which he served until his death in 1611.

Francis and Bridget Marbury had thirteen children, of whom Anne was the second child and the eldest daughter. Marbury sent his sons to Brasenose College, Oxford. He taught his daughters to read and write, contrary to the seventeenth-century conception of a woman's sphere. The extent beyond which Anne Marbury was to traverse the accepted delineation of a woman's sphere was undoubtedly due in large measure to her unusual upbringing and the model of lively rebellion against established authority exemplified by her father.

In spite of his differences with the church, Francis Marbury remained a conformist and reared his children in conformity. His daughter Anne, however, not only embraced Puritanism but also expanded the accepted Puritan ideology into a theology of her own. But that was to come much later in her life.

In 1612, Anne married William Hutchinson, an Alford merchant and an able businessman of increasing fortune, and left her parents' home in London to return to Alford to live.

William's temperament was complementary to Anne's. Anne was high-strung and excited by new ideas. William was placid. He is portrayed by historians as a worthy but unnotable man who followed his wife's leading in spiritual matters.

That he was viewed in this light also by his contemporaries is attested to by the writings of John Winthrop, first governor of the Massachusetts Bay Colony. Winthrop described William Hutchinson as a man of mild temper and weak parts, wholly guided by his wife.

William respected and admired his wife and never questioned her divine revelations. Years later, in exile in Rhode Island with Anne, he was to declare, "I am more tied to my wife than to the church, and I think her to be a dear saint and servant of God." [1] But that time, too, lay far in the future.

For the first twenty-two years of their marriage, the couple resided in Alford, during which time fourteen of their fifteen children were born. (The youngest, Zuriel, was born in Massachusetts in 1636.)

During this period, also, a son and two daughters died—William in infancy, Susanna and Elizabeth in the fall of 1630, within a month of each other. They were apparently victims of the plague of that year. In accordance with the custom of the times, a son born after their son William's death was also named William, and a daughter was named Susanna.

The deaths of her two young daughters seem to have been a factor in Anne Hutchinson's gradual acceptance of the doctrine of the Covenant of Grace, which later came to be the focal point of her theological views.

Anne Hutchinson had a remarkable gift for the practice of medicine. She grew herbs in her garden which she used to distill

medicines and to mix ointments and powders. Coupled with her gift
for medicine, in an age of scant scientific medical knowledge, she had
a gift for nursing, especially midwifery.

In addition, she possessed an unusual faculty for instilling in the
women to whom she ministered a belief in her healing powers which
greatly facilitated the medicinal benefit of the herbs.

The practice of medicine provided an outlet for Anne
Hutchinson's energies, which were not fully dissipated even by the
rigors of housekeeping and childbearing in the seventeenth century.

Anne saw that the pewter shone on the oaken dressers, that the
feather beds were shaken, and that the linen was mended each week
and laundered a few times a year. She supervised the maids at their
spinning and the dairymaid at her churning. She planted her flower
and vegetable gardens. She nursed her babies and comforted
goodwives in child labor. She loved her husband and her children
wholeheartedly, but something within her—a streak of mysticism—
remained unsatisfied.[2]

## Follower

Then John Cotton entered her life.

As the dynamic young vicar of St. Botolph's Church in Boston,
Lincolnshire, the brilliant former head lecturer and dean of
Emmanuel College, Cambridge, soon became a prominent leader of
Puritanism in England. The Puritans had no desire to break with the
established church, that is, the Anglican Church. They only asked
that it be "purified."

Part of what they objected to was the Roman Catholic ritual:
vestments, candles, incense, and readings of the Scripture passages
without priestly interpretation. They also wanted dedicated ministers
who would truly be shepherds of the flock and who would consecrate
their followers by preaching them sermons in plain, understandable
English.

John Cotton publicly declared his intention of casting off the
Romish trappings which still clung to the established church. He had
decided to defy his bishops by dropping all church ceremonies which
had no express warrant from Scripture. These included wearing the
surplice while preaching, making the sign of the cross at baptisms,
and kneeling at Communion. Cotton insisted that these were devices
of the pope, who was Antichrist.

Anne and William Hutchinson often traveled by horseback the

twenty-five miles from their Alford home to Boston, Lincolnshire, to hear this compelling preacher. Anne found in John Cotton her soul mate and spiritual mentor. The two became close friends, mutually supportive of each other. Cotton admired Anne for her barbed wit and keen mind, and he valued her adulation of him as a tribute from a woman capable of forming her own opinions.

For her part, Anne was challenged by John Cotton's sermons and conversations to search the Scriptures for herself and to reexamine her own religious views. As a result, she experienced a dramatic conversion in the form of a divine revelation which came one day, like a brilliant burst of flame, as she was reading a passage from the Song of Solomon.

During the course of the ensuing year, Anne came to the painful conclusion that the ministers of the established church were Antichrist. Even the nonconformist ideology of Puritanism was insufficient for her. Had it not been for John Cotton and John Wheelwright, the brilliant young vicar at nearby Bilsby village who steadfastly defied the established church and later became Anne's brother-in-law and eventually her disciple, her spiritual isolation would have been complete.

In March, 1630, John Cotton journeyed to Southampton to preach the farewell sermon to the Puritan fleet of eleven ships embarking for America with a charter from Charles I for the establishment of the Massachusetts Bay Colony. Four of the ships, carrying four hundred passengers, set sail on March 29. The remainder would follow before the year was out.

Since Puritans were forbidden to leave the country, care had been taken that it not be publicly known that the grant would be used by Puritans. While the leaders would be Puritans, the mass of the colonists would be persons of the middle or lower classes with little or no religious preoccupation. To the Puritans participating in the enterprise, the expedition represented the people Israel embarking for the Promised Land.

John Cotton had participated in the meeting at which plans for the migration had been made. His former fellow student at Trinity College, Cambridge, John Winthrop, also was present at the meeting. In Cotton and Winthrop, respectively, infant church and infant state were personified. Winthrop accepted election to the governorship of the new colony. Cotton was to remain behind in England for as long as he could continue to preach his beliefs.

This turned out to be but a scant two years longer. In 1632 he received a summons to appear before the High Commission. To obey this summons would have meant certain imprisonment. Cotton went into hiding in the London house of John Davenport, there to wait out the winter. In the summer of 1633 he would go to America.

Anne Hutchinson was devastated by this turn of events. Throughout the long winter she was desolate. Then came the revelation with a force that could not be denied: she must follow John Cotton to the wilderness of America.

William had never doubted his wife's revelations. He did not doubt now. The Hutchinsons began to make plans to immigrate to Massachusetts.

They dispatched the two Edward Hutchinsons—the younger, their son, just turned twenty; the elder, William's brother—to sail on the *Griffin,* the ship which would also carry John Cotton and his wife, smuggled aboard, to America. The two Edwards would make the necessary preparations for the Hutchinsons to follow them in 1634.

In May of that year, the Hutchinson family, taking with them Anne's youngest sister, Katharine Marbury, twenty-four years old and an ardent Puritan, boarded the *Griffin,* which had returned to England and was setting sail for another voyage to America.

Anne Hutchinson, age forty-three, quelled an uneasy premonition of impending disaster and turned her face toward Massachusetts.

## Theologian

Accepted at once into the top echelon of Boston society, Anne and William quickly made a place for themselves as leaders in the community. William built a spacious house for his family across the street from Governor John Winthrop's house. William entered the cloth trade and prospered. He was elected a deputy from Boston to the Massachusetts General Court, the highest political authority in the colony.

Anne took on the role of spiritual adviser to others of her sex. As in England, she dispensed her medicinal herbs to ailing women and performed her capable services as midwife. She quickly became the most loved woman in Boston, for again, as in Alford, England, the women to whom she ministered responded to her innate power to sway people by the sheer strength and charm of her personality.

Church attendance was compulsory in the colony, but women

often were kept at home by their own or their children's illnesses. Anne began to hold a weekly evening meeting for women in her home. At first she merely exercised her remarkable memory to repeat the main points of the previous Sunday's sermon. Later she added her own interpretations of the sermon. Gradually she began to expound her own theological views.

Her weekly meetings became so popular with the women that some of the husbands began to accompany their wives. Soon seventy to eighty people were coming to the Hutchinsons' home each week.

To accommodate the increasing numbers, Anne began holding a second weekly meeting for both women and men, in addition to the original meeting for women only. Among those faithful and enthusiastic in attendance were some of Boston's most illustrious citizens.

Even though it was highly unusual for a woman to conduct such meetings and to set herself up as a teacher of men, Anne Hutchinson's meetings probably would have gone uncensured had not her teaching taken a subtle turn. Anne began to question in her own mind the religious views of the ministers of the Massachusetts Bay Colony.

She came to the conclusion, although she could not publicly say so, that with the sole exceptions of John Cotton and John Wheelwright, her brother-in-law, the ministers were not sealed with her conception of grace. Furthermore, she privately decided, they were preaching a Covenant of Works as opposed to a Covenant of Grace.

While for Anne Hutchinson and the founders of New England, Puritanism meant an insistence upon an evangelical ministry of preaching the Word of God, Puritanism nevertheless was deeply rooted in the moral law of the Old Testament, especially the Law of Moses.

Puritan doctrine maintained that a sanctified life was sure evidence of inward grace, a concept that not only provided concrete assurance of election—that is, predestination to eternal life as one of God's elect—but ensured the moral responsibility of the elect. This doctrine was termed a Covenant of Works.

To counteract the legalistic aspect of salvation manifested through works, John Cotton propounded the doctrine of a Covenant of Grace, which held that believers had an intuitive awareness of election. Although believers must always strive to live pure lives, not until they had received the witness of the Spirit were they free to advance their moral condition as a secondary evidence of their state of grace.[3]

Anne Hutchinson not only enthusiastically embraced John Cotton's doctrine of the Covenant of Grace but carried it much further than Cotton ever intended in minimizing the moral responsibility of Christians toward the law. She reasoned that when God extended salvation to a person he placed the Holy Spirit within the person. As a result of this divine action, the Holy Spirit took complete possession of the person's life.

She further concluded that human actions did not provide a clue as to whether or not this transformation had taken place. The fact that a person behaved in a sanctified manner, breaking none of the laws of God, was no evidence that the person was saved. This was in direct contradiction of orthodox Puritan belief. It appeared that Anne Hutchinson was an antinomian.

Antinomianism in its root sense means "against or opposed to the law." In theology it is the doctrine that the moral law is not binding upon Christians, who are under the law of grace. In New England in the 1600s antinomianism denoted the opposition between a person's obedience to the law or the person's works, and the saving grace communicated by the Holy Spirit.

To most seventeenth-century Protestants, including the colonists in Massachusetts, the term "antinomianism" carried with it the stigma of licentious behavior, together with disregard for the law, practiced by those originally designated antinomians. Therefore, the Puritans of Massachusetts, including Anne Hutchinson's disciples, who stood for free grace as opposed to legalistic works, did not call themselves antinomians. Rather, the term was attached to them as a label by those who wished to discredit them.

The Antinomian Controversy, which covered the three-year period from 1636 to 1638 in Massachusetts, was essentially a struggle for control of Massachusetts. When control by the anti-antinomians was assured, the victors showed little mercy to the vanquished. Stiff fines, prison sentences, and banishment were the consequences suffered by many who had openly declared themselves to be Anne Hutchinson's disciples and therefore had been branded antinomians and heretics.

John Wheelwright was banished to the wilderness of New Hampshire as a result of his conviction by the General Court on charges of contempt and sedition. The charges were based on a controversial sermon he had preached in Boston Church, written in collaboration with his sister-in-law. The court ruled that in preaching the sermon he had purposely set himself to kindle and increase bitterness in the colony.

A prominent figure among the Hutchinsonians, as Anne's followers were called, was the young and brilliant Henry Vane. This politically inexperienced young man, by the sheer force of his personality, had charmed the colony into electing him governor, thus defeating the politically astute and powerful John Winthrop.

After serving a brief term from 1636 to 1637, Vane was unseated in a stormy election by Winthrop, who thus regained the governorship. When Vane departed to take care of his personal business affairs in England, Anne lost her most ardent and politically powerful supporter.

With John Wheelwright in exile and Henry Vane in England, Anne Hutchinson stood alone.

## Defendant

Anne Hutchinson was much too astute to label openly the Bay ministers as preachers of a Covenant of Works, an indictment which they vehemently would have denied. But the subtle implications of her weekly prophecies, as they came to be called, left little doubt that she had placed all of them, en masse, with the sole exceptions of John Cotton and John Wheelwright, in this category.

The ministers, to say the least, were far from enamored of this woman who had pronounced this unwelcome judgment upon them. Twice they summoned Anne Hutchinson and John Wheelwright, together with John Cotton, suspected to be the source of Anne's heretical ideas, to a private hearing, encouraging her to speak freely, as among friends. Although the message to desist from her weekly meetings was unmistakable, the irrepressible prophet disregarded the warning and continued her teaching as usual.

Then the blow fell. On November 7, 1637, Anne Hutchinson was summoned to appear before the General Court at Newtowne. Her examination might be compared to a kangaroo court of the twentieth century, for her accusers had already decided upon her guilt before she even appeared in court.

The trial was a near disaster. The defendant, by her calm, well-reasoned responses and quick flashes of wit, made the charges appear ridiculous. To make matters more difficult for her accusers, she had been so astute in her actual utterances that only minor charges could be brought against her.

Because she had not signed the petition drawn up by Wheelwright's supporters in his favor and for which the signers were to be severely punished, she could only be charged with countenancing and supporting those who had signed it.

Another charge was that the weekly meetings she held in her home were neither acceptable to God nor fitting for her sex.

Lastly, she was accused of having "traduced the faithful ministers of the colony."[4]

Anne's quick and ready tongue was more than a match for her accusers. Called upon to justify herself for having assumed the role of teacher, she quoted two passages of Scripture. Upon being told that the passages did not apply to her, she replied, "Must I show my name written therein?"

In gross violation of assurances of confidentiality given at her meetings with the ministers, some of her own statements were used against her. Six of the ministers gave evidence based on the meetings. Anne Hutchinson was quick to point out that her statements were privileged ones and therefore inadmissible as evidence.

Furthermore, she asserted that the ministers' testimonies were an inaccurate account of what had actually transpired at the meetings. She produced a duplicate copy of the notes taken by John Wilson, who along with John Cotton was one of the two ministers of Boston Church, to substantiate her charge. (Wilson, her archenemy, feebly murmured that he had lost his original copy.)

Her vacillating but still loyal ally, John Cotton, delivered a lengthy theological discourse in her defense.

Anne Hutchinson stood on the very brink of acquittal. Then her voluble tongue proved to be her own undoing. In an uncontrollable outburst, she released a torrent of invective, concluding with the claim that a series of divine prophecies had revealed to her, while still in England, that she would suffer many things in New England and that her accusers ultimately were to be destroyed.

Asked how she knew that the Holy Spirit had directed her, she responded, "By an immediate revelation. By the voice of his own Spirit to my soul." This pronouncement testified to something very like the inner light of the Quakers. The Puritans believed that direct revelation had come to an end with the completion of the Bible. This was heresy. She uttered other heresies. She convicted herself.

The court quickly found her guilty as charged and pronounced sentence of banishment from the colony. Because she was in the throes of what was presumed to be a troublesome pregnancy, her sentence was deferred until spring, and she was permitted to pass the winter in house arrest in the home of Joseph Welde in Roxbury.

During the four-month period she was visited, to the point of harassment, by several delegations of Bay ministers and elders of the church, intent upon trapping her in further heresies to justify her excommunication from the church. During this period John Cotton did an about-face and forsook his old friend and follower.

Ill and exhausted, Anne Hutchinson gave forth feverish utterances which were duly noted by her enemies and drawn up in a formal statement of heresies. Soon the ministers had a list of twenty-nine errors upon which to try her for heresy before the congregation of Boston Church.

Her church trial, set for March 15, 1638, was presided over by her former mentor, John Cotton. As had been the case [1] in her examination before the General Court, it appeared that her accusers, rather than she, were on trial. In response to their questions, she confounded the ministers with searching theological questions of her own. Unable to answer her questions, the ministers took refuge in lengthy theological debate.

After two exhausting days of fruitless discussion, the ministers persuaded the congregation, lost in a theological maze, to vote Anne guilty of heresy. Her assertion that she had not held these heretical beliefs prior to her trial and confinement, that they were the result of much morbid, meditative brooding during her months of confinement at Roxbury, and that she was honestly searching for more light went unheeded. When she publicly recanted, she was accused of lying. The edict of excommunication was pronounced.

After her trial, Anne journeyed to Rhode Island to join her husband, William, who had gone ahead to stake out a home at Aquidneck, not far from Roger Williams' colony of dissenters at Providence. There her presumed pregnancy resulted in a "monstrous" birth.

A present-day theory holds that what Anne actually experienced was not a pregnancy at all but a pathological aberration connected with menopause.[5] But in the seventeenth century little was known about that stage of a woman's life since few women, worn out from childbearing, ever reached it.

The twenty-six or twenty-seven pieces of "inhuman monsters" which were the product of the birth were considered by Anne's tormentors in Massachusetts, when they learned of the grisly event, to correspond roughly to the heretical errors charged against her. The phenomenon only served to make Anne's persecutors feel vindicated for their harsh judgment of her.

Following William's death in 1642, Anne took her six youngest children and moved to New York near the present site of Pelham Bay. She purchased a plot of land from the Dutch, who, unknown to her, had never paid the Mohegan Indians their just due for the land. Consequently, the Mohegans considered the Hutchinsons to be squatters on land that belonged to the Indians.

In September, 1643, a group of the Mohegans swooped down upon the Hutchinson farm and massacred all the members of the family except the youngest daughter, Susanna, whom they carried away with them.

Thus ended the life of this magnetic and compelling prophet in the wilderness.

## A Model for Today

Like all mortals, Anne Hutchinson had feet of clay.

This devout and dedicated woman was something of a religious bigot. She not only seemed to believe that her theological position on the doctrine of the Covenant of Grace was the correct one but also apparently considered that only she was qualified to pass judgment on the theological position of others on the issue.

Rather than being a champion of religious liberty, she appears to have been intolerant of all religious beliefs except her own. Her chief concern appears to have been for her own personal religious freedom. Anne Hutchinson's teachings seemed to elevate the believer above external authority and moral restraints. Her opponents believed that such a doctrine might lead to anarchy and destroy the social cohesion which was important to the survival of the colony.[6]

There is no evidence on which to propound a theory of Anne Hutchinson as a precursor of women's rights. On the contrary, it seems logical that the cause of female education may have been impeded by the demonstration of the effect of learning on the female mind as exemplified by Anne Hutchinson.

So much for Anne Hutchinson's weaknesses. What were her strengths?

Anne Hutchinson was her own person. At first content in her weekly meetings merely to repeat the ideas of another—John Cotton's sermons—she reached the point where she felt compelled to articulate her own ideas.

She did not hesitate to defy the status quo. In presuming, as a woman, to instruct a group of men and women, she departed from the accepted norm for her day.

She dared to deviate from the accepted delineation of a woman's place. Her detractors, chief of whom was John Winthrop, claimed that if she had occupied herself with her duties of home and family she would not have had time for theological discussion.

She was not afraid to be considered unfeminine. John Winthrop accused her of trying to be a husband instead of a wife and of leading other women down this unseemly path. She seems to have been disturbed not at all by this unflattering labeling.

She was not reticent about letting her superior intelligence show in an age when it was considered unseemly for a woman to appear to be more intelligent than a man. Her husband's lifelong admiration is evidence that he did not feel threatened by having an intelligent wife, which is a tribute to the self-image of William Hutchinson. Perhaps that also makes him the first recorded example of a liberated man!

In a time when it was popularly believed that women's weaker minds were not strong enough to withstand the strain of profound theological thinking, Anne Hutchinson demonstrated that she could hold her own, and more, with the most respected of men.

Even her self-centered concern for her own religious liberty had positive effects. Her efforts, combined with those of others who sought religious freedom/ for themselves, resulted in a religious diversity in the colonies which proved to be a powerful force in the realization of the principles guaranteed by the First Amendment to the Constitution.[7]

Finally, the life of Anne Hutchinson exemplifies a profound faith in God and a deep belief in the intrinsic worth of all human beings—both male and female—before God.

One writer paid her this tribute:

> All we know about Anne Hutchinson was written by other hands than hers, for the most part by writers whose main purpose was to discredit her. Yet the force of her intelligence and character penetrate the libels and leave us angry with the writers and not with their intended victim.[8]

This is the legacy of Anne Hutchinson, America's first female theologian.

## Questions for Reflection

1. Anne Marbury was strongly influenced by her father. Name the persons who had the greatest influence on the formation of your early views—parents, other relatives, family friends. In what ways did they help to mold your thinking and your self-image?

2. William Hutchinson, a businessman of unquestionable ability, followed his wife's lead in spiritual matters. Is a man less manly because he acknowledges his wife's superior abilities in a certain sphere? Explain.

3. The seventeenth-century Puritans, unable to purify the established church to their satisfaction from within, withdrew and established their own church. Is it always possible to work within established structures to bring about needed reform, or is withdrawal sometimes necessary? Give examples.

4. In Anne Hutchinson's day women were not permitted to speak in congregational meeting. From the vantage point of the twentieth century we smile at this quaint prohibition. Can you draw any parallels between that practice and the situation today in which women are sometimes limited in opportunities to participate in decision making in the church? Justify your answer.

5. Do you believe that God continued to reveal himself in history after the completion of the New Testament and that he reveals himself through individuals or institutions today? Give examples.

6. What models for today do you see in the life of Anne Hutchinson?

# 2

# MISTRESS OF THE MANOR

## Abigail Adams

### (1744-1818)

## Diana

On October 25, 1764, Abigail Smith, daughter of the Congregational minister of Weymouth, Massachusetts, was married to a young lawyer from the neighboring town of Braintree. His name was John Adams.

The good people of the parish shook their heads and murmured what a pity it was that their parson's middle daughter, in taking as her husband a young man of undistinguished family and uncertain future, was marrying beneath her station.

Abigail Smith was only fourteen that summer day in 1759 when her future husband first crossed the parsonage threshold. He was probably brought by his friend Richard Cranch, who was later to marry, in 1761, the eldest Smith daughter, Mary. Of that first meeting with the sisters, young John Adams recorded in his diary, "Polly and Nabby are Wits." [1]

Abigail Smith was reared in a simple, rural setting. Her father, the Reverend William Smith, enjoyed the position of high social standing accorded the Congregational clergy in the Massachusetts Bay Colony. He was a Harvard graduate and came from a long line of well-to-do merchants.

Abigail's mother, Elizabeth, was a Quincy—one of the leading families of the colony—and was related either by blood or by marriage to several other distinguished families.

During her girlhood years Abigail visited often at Mt. Wallaston, a part of Braintree, the home of her maternal grandfather,

Colonel John Quincy. There her lively mind absorbed many ideas from the books in her grandfather's library and from the conversations of many visitors.

Her grandmother taught her many fine points of the more cultivated arts of homemaking. From the perspective of her adult years, Abigail was to look back upon the visits with her grandparents as a valuable contribution to her education.

Life in the Weymouth parsonage was also stimulating. A steady flow of visitors provided an endless source of lively conversation.

Abigail, as well as her sister Mary, three years older, her younger brother, Billy, and her younger sister, Elizabeth, called Betsy, read extensively of the books in their father's library. Abigail even taught herself to read French.

Abigail's interest in literary pursuits was unusual for the times. The basic rudiments of reading and writing, together with enough simple arithmetic to keep household accounts, were considered to be sufficient for female academic education in colonial days. Abigail's education, even though of the self-taught variety, was considerably above the average for girls of the times.

Nevertheless, she never ceased to lament the fact that she was never sent to school because of ill health in childhood; the lack of a formal education was to be one of her lifelong regrets.

Because distance precluded frequent visits, the young people of Abigail and her sister Mary's circle of friends wrote numerous letters to each other to bridge the gap. Letter writing was an amusing pastime, a fine art to be cultivated, whether the writer had anything of importance to say or not.

It was the custom to adopt a pseudonym from ancient history or classical mythology, to be used in place of the writer's real name. Thus, in their courtship years Abigail Smith and John Adams became "Diana" and "Lysander." Goddess of the moon of Roman mythology and the military commander of ancient Sparta seem fitting designations for the young lovers who wrote with a delightfully carefree abandon almost unheard of for the great-grandchildren of the Puritans.

"Miss Adorable" was hardly the standard salutation of a letter, any more than was an order for kisses payable to the bearer on demand a typical ingredient of colonial correspondence. Yet the youthful John Adams addressed such a letter to the daughter of a Congregational minister!

By the time Abigail was sixteen, John Adams was a frequent caller at the parsonage and a lively courtship had developed. Many sparkling letters flew back and forth between the Adamses' farm and the Weymouth parsonage. The young lawyer was recognized by Abigail's parents as their middle daughter's official suitor. In the fall of 1763, when Abigail was eighteen and John was twenty-seven, the pair became engaged.

John Adams came from a family background of small farmers. Four generations earlier, in 1636, his ancestor, Henry Adams, had immigrated from England to escape religious persecution. Henry's eighteenth-century descendants were of solid but unnotable stock.

In accordance with the custom of the times in families which could afford to send only one son to college, John Adams, as the eldest, received the Harvard education. To even matters out a bit, his younger brothers, Peter and Elihu, at their father's death in 1761, received the bulk of the family estate.

Even so, John received a portion of the inheritance, which consisted of a saltbox cottage across the way from the main house and several acres of farmland and timberland. This modest inheritance, together with his steadily growing law practice, was sufficient to put his financial affairs on a firm footing. By the fall of 1763, when he became engaged to Abigail, he could afford to marry.

The spring of 1764 brought the outbreak of a widespread epidemic of smallpox in Boston in which a shocking number of people died. Because his law practice required him to ride the court circuits throughout the colony, John Adams decided that a wise course to follow was inoculation against the dread disease.

Vaccination as it is known today not yet having been perfected, inoculation consisted of being infected with the disease, under controlled conditions, and then spending several weeks recuperating in a "hospital," usually a private home. Often several persons were confined at the same time. In April, 1764, John Adams undertook this treatment, necessitating the postponement of his marriage.

Like young lovers since time immemorial, the pair found the separation hard to endure. They sought consolation through pouring out their loneliness in letters to each other, a practice of long standing that served them well during the enforced separation, which was to be but the first of many in the long years ahead.

John wrote:

But the dear Partner of all my Joys and sorrows, in whose

Affections, and Friendship I glory, more than in all other Emoluments under Heaven, comes into my Mind very often and makes me sigh.[2]

Abigail replied:

I am very fearful that you will not when left to your own managment follow your directions—but let her who tenderly cares for you both in Sickness and Health, intreet you to be careful of that Health upon which depends the happiness of Your

A. Smith.[3]

John Adams felt great apprehension that his letters might carry the smallpox germs and infect the young woman he loved with the deadly disease. Even though he himself smoked the letters before sending them, he implored her to be sure that Tom, the family manservant, smoked the letters again to rid them of germs before she touched them. He need not have worried. Abigail's mother was even more solicitous than her lover, to the point that Abigail feared that the letters might suffer total extinction from the smoking!

The five-weeks' ordeal finally over, the lovers were reunited. In the golden autumn they were wed.

## Homemaker

John Adams took his bride to live in the saltbox cottage in Braintree, which was to be their home for the next twenty-four years. John's mother and brothers lived in the family homestead opposite the cottage. Abigail had a warm and loving relationship with her husband's family.

John Adams carved a door from a window in a ground-floor room in the cottage and set up an office for his law practice. However, he was often away from home, riding the court circuits and attending to business affairs in Boston, thirty miles away. Now, as in their courtship years, letters bridged these short-term separations between John and Abigail.

Within a short time after their marriage, the couple experienced the joys of parenthood. Their first child, a daughter, was born the July following their marriage. They named her Abigail and called her Nabby, to distinguish her from her mother.

Two years later, they had a son, whom they named John Quincy after Abigail's grandfather Quincy, the colonel, who had died just before his namesake's birth.

Daughter number two was named Susanna, after John Adams's mother, and was given the pet name Suky. In one of his letters from

Boston, John Adams entreated his wife to "kiss my little Suky, for me."[4] But little Suky was a sickly child from birth, and her life span was to be only fourteen months in length. At her death, her parents experienced the anguish of trying to fathom the meaning of the death of a child lent to them for such a little while and then so quickly snatched away.

Two more sons completed the family: Charles and Thomas Boylston, whose middle name was the family name of John Adams's mother, Susanna Boyleston Adams.

Between 1768 and 1774, the family moved back and forth several times between Braintree and Boston, living in a succession of rented houses. Finally, weary of living in houses belonging to someone else, John Adams purchased a house on Queen Street which became home for the remainder of the family's residence in Boston.

But it was to the cottage in Braintree that the family always returned.

To support his growing family, John Adams was kept busy. To preside over her lively household of husband, children, and servants, Abigail Adams was kept bustling. It was a good and satisfying life. But for the intervening hand of history, the family might have lived out their collective lives contentedly and obscurely in the ageless cycle of birth, life, and death.

But the hand of history did intervene!

Increasing unrest and discontent pervaded the colonies of the middle 1760s and the early 1770s. A series of legislative acts passed by the British Parliament fanned the flames of impending rebellion. The Sugar Act in 1764, the Stamp Act in 1765, and the Townshend Acts in 1767 each had a different provision, but all added up to the same end result: taxation without representation.

The blatant disregard by Parliament of the rights of the colonies led to the formation of Committees of Correspondence in individual colonies to protest taxation without representation. In Massachusetts, John Adams's fiery cousin, Samuel, was the chief organizer of the revolutionary Sons of Liberty.

In 1770, in a minor street disturbance, five men were killed by a small contingent of British soldiers. Spurred by the fiery Samuel, the Sons of Liberty exaggerated the episode out of all proportion and termed it the "Boston Massacre." John Adams succeeded in securing the postponement of the trial of Captain Prescott and the twelve British soldiers under his command until public agitation had died down somewhat and public sentiment became more favorable for the conduct of an impartial trial.

John Adams consented to be the attorney for the defense when others convinced him that in him alone lay the only hope of Captain Prescott and his soldiers for a fair trial. Adams won the case, gaining the acquittal of all the defendants save two, who were branded on the thumb and then released.

It was a tribute to John Adams's public image as a man of integrity that neither his reputation nor his law practice suffered one iota from his defense of this unpopular case.

After this incident came the ultimate injury to the well-being of the colonists: the Tea Act of 1773. To deprive American colonists of their tea in the 1770s was the equivalent of depriving their descendants two centuries later of their coffee.

Masquerading as Indians in the dark of night, a party of colonists (strongly suspected but never actually proven to be the Sons of Liberty led by the hotheaded Samuel Adams) boarded several ships anchored in Boston Harbor and dumped the entire cargo of tea into the Boston Bay.

After this Boston Tea Party, the clamor for separation from England became too insistent to be any longer ignored. The call went out through the colonies summoning delegates to a Congress of the Colonies in Philadelphia.

At considerable mental anguish, John Adams had reached the conclusion that his conscience compelled him to give up his law practice to enter public service. When he received the news that he had been elected a delegate from Massachusetts to the Congress of the Colonies, he accepted the assignment.

In August, 1774, he set out for Philadelphia and what was later to be called the First Continental Congress. It was to be ten years, except for brief intervals, before he again lived at home with his family.

The first ten years of the marriage of John and Abigail, which had passed happily and uneventfully, had come to an end. The long years of separation had begun.

## Portia

Abigail Smith Adams had always been an independent thinker. Even her courtship letters reflected this fact. She was interested in public events of the day and pondered them thoughtfully.

She, too, along with her husband and many others, was deeply disturbed by the growing rift between the colonies and England. As relations gradually worsened, Abigail Adams called for separation from England long before such a stand was the popular position. Eventually her husband reached the same conclusion, but his wife arrived there first.

This marked the beginning of a pattern that was to last a lifetime. Although in all the major issues Abigail Adams's opinions paralleled those of her husband, she arrived at hers independently of him. Far from reflecting her husband's thinking, her conclusions often anticipated his.

So when John Adams decided to relinquish the practice of law for public service, his wife concurred in his decision. Unlike many wives of her own and later times, Abigail Adams understood why her husband had to do what he did.

Letters became more important than ever before in welding the bond between the wife at home in Braintree and the husband in faraway Philadelphia. In Abigail's letters, the custom of a pseudonym was revived. The Diana of the carefree courtship years became the Portia of responsible married life. While John Adams, having discarded the romantic designation of Lysander, never took another pseudonym, he considered the name of Shakespeare's celebrated female lawyer a fitting appellation for his capable wife.

For her part, Abigail considered the designation of "friend" to be the most desirable in all the world. The man to whom she was married was not only husband and lover but also the "Dearest Friend" to whom she addressed her letters and with whom she shared her life.

To both of them, their marriage was a partnership. John Adams, in a point of view far ahead of his time, considered his wife truly his partner in the marriage, fully his equal in intelligence and capabilities. He always considered her—as he had in that first separation in 1764—the "dear Partner of all my Joys and sorrows."

Ten years after that first separation, perhaps in a spasm of conscience at leaving her alone to shoulder the triple burden of house, farm, and family, John Adams reaffirmed that fact in a letter from Philadelphia: "I must intreat you, my dear Partner in all the Joys and Sorrows, Prosperity and Adversity of my Life, to take a part with me in the Struggle." 5

Perhaps it was this easy camaraderie that had always characterized their relationship which made it possible for Abigail

Adams to write her now-famous letter to John Adams at the Second Continental Congress on March 31, 1776, when a declaration of an independency, as it was termed, seemed close at hand:

> I long to hear that you have declared an independancy—[wrote this spirited woman] and by the way in the Code of Laws which I suppose it will be necessary for you to make I desire you would Remember the Ladies, and be more generous and favourable to them than your ancestors. . . . Remember all Men would be tyrants if they could. If perticular care and attention is not paid to the Laidies we are determined to foment a Rebelion, and will not hold ourselves bound by any Laws in which we have no voice, or Representation.
>
> That your Sex are naturally tyrannical is a Truth so thoroughly established as to admit of no dispute, [here we can imagine the quill pen poised in mid-air as the writer suddenly recalled to whom she wrote] but such of you as wish to be happy willingly give up the harsh title of Master for the more tender and endearing one of Friend.[6]

John Adams responded to his wife's unusual demands in a bantering tone:

> As to Declarations of Independency, be patient. . . .
>
> As to your extraordinary Code of Laws, I cannot but laugh. We have been told that our Struggle has loosened the bands of Government every where. That Children and Apprentices were disobedient—that schools and Colledges were grown turbulent—that Indians slighted their Guardians and Negroes grew insolent to their Masters. But your Letter was the first Intimation that another Tribe more numerous and powerfull than all the rest were grown discontented.—This is rather too course a Compliment but you are so saucy, I wont blot it out.
>
> Depend upon it. We know better that to repeal our Masculine systems. Altho they are in full Force, you know they are little more than Theory. We dare not exert our Power in its full Latitude. We are obliged to go fair, and softly, and in Practice you know We are the subjects. We have only the Name of Masters, and rather than give up this, which would compleatly subject Us to the Despotism of the Peticoat, I hope General Washington, and all our brave Heroes would fight.[7]

Thus ran the Abigail—John version of the Great Debate which continues to this day. There is no way of knowing how many women in the thirteen colonies might have shared Abigail Adams's sentiments. Perhaps there were many. But the colonies were widely scattered, travel was difficult, and there was no chain of communication by which women could unite in a common cause. No rebellion was fomented, the moment passed, and the opportunity was lost.

## "Farmeress"

Upon her husband's departure for Philadelphia, Abigail was left with sole responsibility for four small children, the oldest not yet ten years old. In addition to her previous roles of mother to her children and mistress of her household, Abigail assumed the roles of supervisor of the farm, keeper of the family finances, manager of her husband's business affairs, and teacher in charge of the children's education.

She rose to meet these new responsibilities with typical aplomb. She bought and sold farm stock, hired help, and purchased pieces of farmland and timberland advantageously. She dealt with tenants when Braintree, including the Adams homestead, was overrun with refugees from war-torn Boston. She worried over whether to rent the house in Boston or sell it, paid the bills, and practiced the policy of rigid economy urged by her husband.[8]

Not only did Abigail have to run her household and the farm but she also had to run them with inadequate help. It was difficult to keep good servants. After the fighting began, they kept running off to the war!

Not the least of Abigail's frustrations were the shortages of small, everyday items that make up life's necessities. On one occasion she implored her husband to send her pins from Philadelphia. At another time she requested him to send her some writing paper because she had enough for only one more letter. Dress goods were hard to find.

In short, Abigail Adams coped.

In April, 1776, with almost two years' experience behind her, Abigail wrote to John that she hoped to acquire a reputation of being as good a "farmeress" as her partner had of being a good statesman.

John Adams, for his part, took great pride in his wife's business acumen and came to depend upon it more and more. He wrote her teasingly, "I begin to be jealous, that our Neighbours will think Affairs more discreetly conducted in my absence than at any other Time."[9]

There is little doubt that Abigail's managerial skills saved John Adams from the financial ruin of other statesmen of the times, who were rewarded for their public service by being grossly underpaid if, at times, indeed, they were paid at all.

Since Braintree was a scant thirty miles from Boston, the war was literally at Abigail's doorstep. She wrote, "—the constant roar of the cannon is so [distre]ssing that we can not Eat, Drink or Sleep." [10]

One day she took her seven-year-old son, John Quincy, by the hand and walked with him to the top of nearby Penn's Hill to watch the flames of burning Charlestown in the distance.

In August, 1775, an epidemic of dysentery swept over the Boston area, so devastating that Abigail wrote that the desolation of war was not as bad as the havoc wrought by the pestilence. In some cases entire families were wiped out. John Adams's youngest brother, Elihu, was one of the first victims.

John Adams, in Massachusetts during a brief recess of the Second Continental Congress, had no sooner departed for Philadelphia than his entire household was stricken, from his wife to Patty, the servant girl. The Adamses' house became one big hospital.

With the eventual recovery of the immediate family, a new concern arose. Abigail's mother was stricken. In a letter to her husband Abigail wrote that her mother had a premonition that she was not going to get well. Abigail expressed great anxiety that the premonition might prove to be well-founded.

Abigail's next letter to John is written from the Weymouth parsonage on October 1. So agitated is the writer that the customary salutation "Dearest Friend" is forgotten. She plunges directly into the message:

> Have pitty upon me, have pitty upon me o! thou my beloved for the Hand of God presseth me soar.
> Yet will I be dumb and silent and not open my mouth becaus thou o Lord hast done it.
> How can I tell you (o my bursting Heart) that my Dear Mother has Left me, this day about 5 oclock she left this world for an infinitely better.
> After sustaining 16 days severe conflict nature fainted and she fell asleep. Blessed Spirit where art thou? At times I almost am ready to faint under this severe and heavy Stroke, seperated from *thee* who used to be a comfortar towards me in affliction, but blessed be God, his Ear is not heavy that he cannot hear, but he has bid us call upon him in times of Trouble.
> I know you are a sincere and hearty mourner with me and will pray for me in my affliction. My poor father like a firm Believer and a Good christian sets before his children the best of Examples of patience and submission. My sisters send their Love to you and are greatly afflicted. You often Express'd your anxiety for me when you left me before, surrounded with Terrors, but my trouble then was as the small dust in the balance compaird to what I have since endured. I hope to be properly mindful of the correcting hand, that I may not be rebuked in anger.—

You will pardon and forgive all my wanderings of mind. I cannot be correct.

Tis a dreadful time with this whole province. Sickness and death are in almost every family. I have no more shocking and terible Idea of any Distemper except the Plague than this.

Almighty God restrain the pestilence which walketh in darkness and wasteth at noon day and which has laid in the dust one of the dearest of parents. May the Life of the other be lengthened out to his afflicted children and Your distressed

Portia.[11]

But life must go on, as Abigail Adams well knew. Her children needed her, the farm must be looked after, and mourning must give way to the resumption of life's responsibilities. And so the weeks passed, and the months lengthened into years. John Adams continued to sit with the Second Continental Congress in Philadelphia, returning to Braintree to be with his family whenever he could.

In July, 1777, another heartbreak occurred, one which affected the entire family: the stillbirth of a child. Abigail named the tiny, lifeless form Elizabeth, in memory of her mother.

"My Heart was much set upon a Daughter,"[12] Abigail told her husband when she was able to write. She had felt that her desire would be granted, as it was, though fruitlessly.

John Adams responded in thankfulness to God that his "best Friend" had been not only spared but restored to perfect health. He expressed a strange sense of wonder that he could feel such a strong affection for an infant he would never see.

Twelve-year-old Nabby wept for hours over the stillbirth of her little sister. "My dear little Nabbys Tears," commented her father upon being told, "are sweetly becoming her generous Tenderness and sensibility of Nature."[13]

## Hostess

Later that same year, John Adams was appointed to a three-member joint commission to France. He sailed in November, taking with him ten-year-old John Quincy. The joint commission was dissolved the following year, and father and son returned home.

Almost immediately, John Adams was elected minister to negotiate treaties with Britain, and once again sailed for France. This time he took both Johnny and Charley. But taking Charley turned out to be a serious mistake. The nine-year-old boy became acutely homesick, and his father was compelled to send him home.

After a five-year separation, Abigail and Nabby, now nineteen, joined John Adams in Paris. For eight months they lived at Auteuil, just outside the city, and Abigail became mistress of a mansion in which forty beds could be made and which required eight servants to maintain it.

Then John Adams was appointed the first American minister to the Court of St. James, and the family became, in 1785, the first to reside in the American Embassy in London's Grosvenor Square. Although Abigail Adams adjusted to English society, she never became enamored of it, and found a snub by Queen Charlotte, consort of George III, almost impossible to forgive.

She much preferred the simple Congregationalist values of Braintree to the royal pomp of London. At the end of three years, her husband's work completed (not too successfully), she was happy to return home.

From England, John Adams had arranged the purchase of a larger house in Braintree, the saltbox cottage having shrunk considerably in size after the mansions of Auteuil and London. John Adams christened the new house "Peacefield," after the peace he had helped to negotiate and in the expectation that the house would provide a peaceful haven from the cares and pressures of public life.

Peacefield was to be the family home for the remainder of John and Abigail's life together. During John Adams's two terms as the first Vice-President and one term as the second President of the United States, Abigail alternated her residence between Peacefield and New York, the nation's first capital, and later between Peacefield and the second capital, Philadelphia.

Abigail missed her husband's inauguration as President of the United States in order to be with her dying mother-in-law in Massachusetts, but she wrote him this letter:

> . . . You have this day to declare yourself head of a nation. "And now, O Lord, my God, Thou hast made thy servant ruler over the people. Give unto him an understanding heart, that he may know how to go out and come in before this great people; that he may discern between good and bad. . . ."
>
> My thoughts and my meditations are with you, though personally absent; and my petitions to Heaven are that "the things which make for peace may not be hidden from your eyes." My feelings are not those of pride or ostentation upon the occasion. They are solemnized by a sense of the obligations, the important trusts, and numerous duties connected

with it. That you may be enabled to discharge them with honor to yourself, with justice and impartiality to your country, and with satisfaction to the great people, shall be the daily prayer of your
A.A.[14]

Abigail Adams had the somewhat dubious distinction of being the first First Lady to live in the new President's House on the Potomac (it was not called the White House until many years later) in the new city of Washington. After the pleasant, comfortable mansions of Richmond Hill in New York and Bush Hill in Philadelphia, the damp, cavernous rooms of the uncompleted "castle," as it was termed by Abigail, were far from appealing.

Thirteen fires were required daily to ward off the penetrating chill. The resourceful Abigail hung the family wash in the East Room. She soon turned the shell of a house into an inviting home for the three remaining months of her husband's presidency.

In March, 1801, John Adams having been defeated for a second term by Thomas Jefferson, John and Abigail retired to Peacefield in Quincy (as Braintree had been renamed.). There Abigail spent eighteen good years as the matriarch who held together her large and widely scattered family through her life-long habit of writing numerous letters.

Josiah Quincy, a neighbor and relative, years later recorded his remembrance as a six-year-old boy of Sunday dinners in the Adamses' home:

> . . . the genuine kindness of the President, who had not the smallest chip of an iceberg in his composition, soon made me perfectly at ease in his society. With Mrs. Adams there was a shade more formality. A consciousness of age and dignity, which was often somewhat oppressive, was customary with old people of that day in the presence of the young. Something of this Mrs. Adams certainly had, though it wore off or came to be disregarded by me, for in the end I was strongly attached to her. She always dressed handsomely, and her rich silks and laces seemed appropriate to a lady of her dignified position in the town. If there was a little savor of patronage in the generous hospitality she exercised among her simple neighbors, it was never regarded as more than a natural emphasis of her undoubted claims to precedence.[15]

Abigail Adams did not live to see her son John Quincy Adams become the sixth President of the United States, but his appointment as President James Monroe's Secretary of State was the crowning glory of her life.[16]

On October 25, 1814, Abigail and her partner of fifty years

celebrated their golden wedding anniversary, a more notable achievement in the early nineteenth century than it is today.

Four years later, John Adams scrawled an agitated message to his old friend Thomas Jefferson: "The dear Partner of my Life, for fifty four Years as a Wife and for many Years more as a Lover, now Lyes in extremis, forbidden to speak or be spoken to." [17]

Abigail had suffered a stroke, followed by typhoid fever.

Abigail Adams died on October 28, 1818. On November 11, she would have been seventy-four years old.

Eliza Susan Quincy, another neighbor and relative, recorded in her journal:

> Our excellent friend Mrs. Abigail Adams died today. For several days we had given up all hope of her recovery but this preparation did not render the event less affecting to us all. Her place can never be filled in society. Advanced as she was in life, that life was never more useful and valuable to those around her than when she cheerfully resigned it. For many days she was unable to converse with her friends. But the day before her death she sent for Mr. Adams, and had a long conversation with him, said she was resigned and willing to depart, and entreated him to support their separation with firmness and evince his Faith,—by fortitude on her loss.
>
> When our privileges are withdrawn we feel as if we had not justly estimated their value, but I shall ever remember with gratitude that of having enjoyed the society of this excellent and remarkable woman, and notwithstanding the difference in our ages, I have in some degree appreciated the advantages to be derived from her experienced conversation. Her place is in History—she will never be forgotten.[18]

Her husband survived their final separation by eight years.

## A Model for Today

It in no way detracts from Abigail Adams's strengths to admit that she had points of weakness. Rather, her weaknesses make her seem more human and her strengths more believable.

Abigail Adams was a meddling mother. There is evidence that she interfered with the romantic interests of her daughter, Nabby, and her son, John Quincy, with the result that both relinquished their first choices and married other mates.

In Nabby's case, Abigail achieved her end not so much by actively opposing the suit of young Royall Tyler, far away in Braintree, as by subtly promoting the cause of the handsome and dashing Colonel William Stephens Smith, John Adams's Secretary of Legation in London. When Nabby and the colonel were married in

Grosvenor Square, there was much rejoicing. But Royall Tyler moved on to a successful career while Colonel Smith's ill-reasoned business ventures were to be an endless source of anxiety and uneasiness to John and Abigail during all the years of Nabby and the colonel's marriage.

Abigail loved her children wholeheartedly, but she could not refrain from dispensing liberal portions of unsolicited advice and admonitions to them even in their adult years. Fortunately, they seem to have accepted this characteristic of their mother in good grace.

Abigail was something of a nagging wife. Her letters contain many reproaches to her husband for not writing as often as she would wish and for not writing longer letters than he did. There is ample evidence that John Adams found this one trait of his wife hard to handle.

Abigail Adams found it difficult to forgive an injury, either to herself or to someone she loved. Years after the London experience, she spoke with some asperity of Charlotte, and felt that the Queen of England well deserved all of the adversities which life had brought to her.

She was less willing than her husband to forgive Thomas Jefferson, who had been a close friend to both of them during the Paris and London years but who later became John Adams's political adversary. Years later, in retirement at Quincy, John Adams effected a warm reconciliation with his former friend through a mutually satisfying correspondence which brightened the last years of both men. Abigail eventually followed the same path, but she was slower than her husband to forgive and forget past injuries.

Abigail Adams was to the extreme a partisan of her husband's policies as president. She tended to equate opposition to her husband's policies with treason against the government.

But her strengths by far outweighed her weaknesses.

Abigail Adams had a deep religious faith which sustained her through many personal griefs. Her mother's death in the war years had been a heavy blow, but there were more to follow.

Her son Charley, failing to fulfill the bright promise he had shown as a boy, died an alcoholic at the age of thirty, leaving a wife and two young daughters.

Her daughter Nabby, stricken with cancer, was taken to her parents' home in Quincy in the futile hope that medical treatment available in Massachusetts would help her. Nabby died in 1813, at the age of forty-eight, leaving two sons and her daughter, Caroline, as well as her husband, the colonel.

The deaths of her children were grievous blows to Abigail, but the guiding philosophy of her life, "Shall we receive good and not evil?" was more than theory. She once wrote her sister, Mary Cranch, "Who of us pass through the world with our path strewed with flowers, without encountering the thorns?" [19]

Abigail Adams had a strong sense of family. She brought up three grandchildren: Caroline, Nabby's daughter, and Susanna and Abigail, Charley's daughters. For several years she had in her home her niece, Louisa Smith, her brother William's daughter. The fact that she missed her husband's inauguration as President of the United States to be at her mother-in-law's side in her final illness illustrates the depth of affection she felt for her husband's mother.

Perhaps it was this same sense of family that enabled Abigail, when she and Nabby joined John Adams in Paris, to entrust her sons Charley and Tommy to the keeping of her sister Betsy and her husband, the Reverend William Shaw, confident that they would be well cared for and well educated.

Abigail Adams believed in her own capabilities. Without arrogance or false pride but also without false modesty, she matter-of-factly considered herself capable of assuming the many roles thrust upon her by an unforeseeable twist of circumstances. She was not afraid to accept responsibility. She simply saw what needed to be done and did it.

While she considered herself an equal partner with her husband, she did not try to "take over." She consulted him about matters which required a joint decision, as on the question of what to do about their house in Boston.

Abigail Adams desired for other women what she had for herself. When she admonished her husband to "remember the ladies," she was speaking in behalf of others as well as for herself.

She was ahead of her time in advocating education for girls. When, of necessity, she became her children's teacher, she educated her daughter along with her sons, contrary to the thinking of the times.

The type of man to whom she was married, combined with the circumstances of the times in which she lived, enabled her to employ her unique talents and capabilities in a way that was satisfying and fulfilling. She was able to function fully as an individual.

The outstanding model that the life of Abigail Adams offers is the shining fact that she unmistakably enjoyed being what she was. She liked being a wife, a mother, and a homemaker. She liked her role in life. She was happy with her lot.

One of the benefits to future generations which resulted from the long and trying separations between John and Abigail Adams was the blossoming of Abigail's natural gifts as a letter writer. Today her letters are valued by historians because of the fresh and natural picture they paint of life in colonial and revolutionary times. She had opinions on topics great and small and expressed them spontaneously and indiscriminately in her letters. The voluminous correspondence which she left consists of a delightful mixture of the profound and the mundane.

The world would be a poorer place without Abigail Adams's letters. The world would have been a poorer place without Abigail Adams.

## Questions for Reflection

1. A biography of Abigail Adams must of necessity also be a biography of John Adams. Is it necessarily bad when the life of a wife is inseparably bound up with that of her husband? What are some things a wife can do to maintain her own identity?

2. The unforeseeable twist of circumstances which resulted in her husband's prolonged absences from home drew forth from Abigail Adams latent reserves of resourcefulness and inner strength. Recall some occasions in which you had to draw from deep within yourself initiatives and capabilities you had not known you possessed. In what ways did such experiences contribute to your growth?

3. Abigail and John Adams were separated by great distances and for prolonged periods of time for many years of their married life. Yet their marriage was an exceptionally good one, solid and stable. What factors can you identify as having contributed to making their marriage such an outstanding one? What parallels can you draw to marriages of today?

4. Abigail Adams found it difficult to be reconciled to Thomas Jefferson because he had opposed her husband. Have you ever found it more difficult to forgive an injury to someone you love than to yourself? How did you deal with the situation?

5. Abigail Adams was one of the most prolific letter writers of all time. Today letter writing has become largely a lost art. The telephone, jet travel, and the fast pace of living have been significant factors in the demise of the personal letter. Do you believe that the rapidly increasing mobility of our society, resulting in separation from friends and family, may bring about a resurgence of letter writing? Why or why not?

6. What models for today do you see in the life of Abigail Adams?

# 3
# REBELS WITH A CAUSE

*The Grimké Sisters*

| Sarah | Angelina |
|-------|----------|
| *(1792-1873)* | *(1805-1879)* |

## Sarah

The lives of Sarah and Angelina Grimké were so intertwined that the sisters functioned as an inseparable unit. Sarah was the sixth and Angelina the last of the fourteen children of an illustrious Charleston, South Carolina, family.

The Grimké sisters were an unusual phenomenon: Southern abolitionists. The fact that they were women, as well as Southerners, was an additional element in the public sensation they created as active participants in the antislavery movement in the North preceding the Civil War.

Sarah Moore Grimké, born on November 26, 1792, possessed the seeking mind that often accompanies a keen intelligence. The education considered sufficient for a girl in the early nineteenth century was completely inadequate for a girl of Sarah's superior intellect. The "good education" she received in a private school for the daughters of wealthy Charleston families consisted of reading, writing, simple arithmetic, and a little French, together with needlework, drawing, and music.

Deprived of academic studies of any depth at school, Sarah studied her brother Thomas's lessons in history, geography, science, mathematics, and even Greek. When Thomas undertook the study of Latin and Sarah sought permission to study along with him, however, she met with opposition on all fronts. Her father disapproved; her mother considered the idea preposterous; and even Thomas, usually her ally, forsook her. Deeply disappointed, Sarah abandoned the idea.

Sarah longed to be a lawyer. Her father recognized her exceptional mental ability and conceded that she would have made the best jurist in the country—if she had only been a boy. But she was a girl, and for a girl, studying law was unthinkable.

And so Thomas was sent away to study law at Yale, and Sarah was kept at home to learn the social graces so important to young ladies of families of high social standing.

The Grimké family ranked in the top echelon of Charleston society. The father, John Faucheraud Grimké, who had served as a lieutenant colonel in the Revolutionary War, was from a wealthy and distinguished family of French Huguenot stock. By the time his children were born, he had become a judge on the South Carolina Supreme Court and was a part of the ruling elite of the state. The mother, Mary Smith Grimké, was of illustrious Irish and English-Puritan ancestry. Her father was one of the wealthiest and most respected men in South Carolina.

Like other wealthy families, the Grimkés owned several plantations and also maintained a townhouse in Charleston. They alternated their residence, according to the season, between the Charleston townhouse and the plantation outside Beaufort. Several hundred slaves performed the labor necessary for the operation of these extensive establishments.

From early childhood Sarah Grimké displayed a deep sensitivity to the plight of the slaves. At the age of four she inadvertently witnessed the whipping of a slave for some minor offense. Her nurse found her later at the harbor pleading with the captain of one of the ships to take her away to a place where such dreadful things did not happen.

From that time on, when the little girl knew that a slave was about to be punished, she always prayed that somehow the punishment would be averted, and she shed many tears when her prayers were not successful.

Early in life Sarah learned about the workhouse in Charleston. There medieval forms of torture were meted out as punishment to slaves whose masters willingly paid others to inflict the punishment they themselves were too squeamish to administer.

Sarah Grimké owned only one slave in her life, a little girl close to her own age whom she treated more like a playmate than a servant. When the girl died, the little mistress was inconsolable and refused ever to accept another slave. She finally consented, upon her mother's urging, at the age of twelve, to accept the services of a waiting-maid. Like other daughters of wealthy families, Sarah attended Episcopal church services on Sunday mornings and taught a Sunday school class for Negro children on Sunday afternoons. She soon became frustrated because the lessons had to be completely oral. South Carolina law forbade teaching Negroes to read or write. Sarah could not accept the rationale that knowing how to read would make the slaves rebellious. She undertook to teach her waiting-maid to read. She later recorded in her diary:

> . . . my great desire in this matter would not be totally suppressed, and I took an almost malicious satisfaction in teaching my little waiting-maid at night, when she was supposed to be occupied in combing and brushing my long locks. The light was put out, the keyhole screened, and flat on our stomachs before the fire, with the spelling-book under our eyes, we defied the laws of South Carolina.[1]

The dreadful crime was discovered. The little maid barely escaped a whipping, but the greater burden of guilt was laid upon the mistress. Summoning her into his presence, Judge Grimké sternly impressed upon his daughter the enormity of her misconduct. From that time on, Sarah outwardly conformed to circumstances. However, the fires of inner rebellion, though reduced to smoldering coals, were far from extinguished.

It was at this point in Sarah's life that Angelina was born. Smarting from the injustice of being denied the opportunity to study law and nursing her intense disappointment in the realization that she was powerless to help the slaves, Sarah, almost thirteen years old, eagerly found in the new baby a purpose for her life. She persuaded her parents to permit her to be godmother to Angelina.

The elder sister took almost complete charge of the younger one. Sarah gave Angelina the pet name "Nina," and Angelina called her older sister "Mother." This relationship endured throughout their lives.

At the age of sixteen Sarah entered Charleston society. She attended parties and in general was caught up in the social whirl enjoyed by the young people her age. She escaped making a hasty marriage only by the intervention of her brother Thomas.

Then she was converted in a revival meeting and gave up the frivolous pastimes enjoyed by her fashionable set. She backslid, returned to the fold, backslid again, returned to the fold again, in a continuous cycle. She never seemed to find what she was looking for.

When she was twenty-six, her father became ill, and Sarah convinced herself that she was to blame for her father's illness because of her sinful ways. She attempted to purge herself of guilt by taking upon herself the complete care of her father. When the Charleston doctors advised a trip to Philadelphia to consult a well-known surgeon there, Judge Grimké chose Sarah, of all his sons and daughters, to accompany him.

The consultation in Philadelphia proved futile. The doctor could only suggest that the fresh ocean breezes of the New Jersey shore might prove beneficial to the patient. The closest the judge ever got to the ocean, however, was the view from his window. After a few weeks of suffering, with his daughter keeping solitary vigil at his bedside, Judge Grimké died.

In Charleston the judge would have been accorded a funeral accompanied by much pomp. In Long Branch, New Jersey, there was no one but his daughter to walk behind his coffin in the funeral procession.

After her father's death, Sarah returned to Philadelphia and for two months boarded in the household of a Quaker family. She returned to Charleston by boat, and during the voyage spent some time with a group of Quakers, one of whom was Israel Morris, a highly respected and well-to-do merchant. He gave Sarah a copy of the works of the noted Quaker, John Woolman, and invited her to write him with any questions she might have about Quakerism.

Sarah returned home a changed person. During all the weeks in Philadelphia and Long Branch, she had had the sole responsibility for her father's care, without even a servant to share the load. Her father had demonstrated his implicit trust in his daughter's ability to assume complete charge of a difficult situation. As a result of the whole experience, Sarah acquired a sense of self-confidence and self-worth that never left her.

Sarah became increasingly drawn to the Quaker faith. She read Woolman and wrote to Israel Morris requesting additional reading matter on Quakerism.

Finally, one day, Sarah announced to her family that she was going to Philadelphia to live and become a Quaker. Her family was scandalized at the idea. In 1821 a young woman, even though she was twenty-eight years old, did not live on her own, and she certainly did not set out alone for a strange city.

Sarah was resolute. She would not be dissuaded. Her younger

sister, Anna Frost, widowed after only a year of marriage and left with a baby daughter, agreed to accompany Sarah to Philadelphia. Anna's chaperonage made the arrangement more respectable in the eyes of society and more acceptable to the family.

Although she would return for several brief visits, Charleston would never be home to Sarah Grimké again.

When Sarah and Anna arrived in Philadelphia, Anna found living quarters for herself and her daughter and Sarah stayed for a time in the home of Israel Morris, his charming wife, and their eight children. Sarah joined the Society of Friends and soon felt called to be a Quaker minister. But her delivery was halting and stiff and made an unfavorable impression. For this reason her petition was repeatedly denied.

Israel Morris became widowed, and in the course of time he asked Sarah to marry him. Sarah, although deeply in love with him, refused his proposal, for reasons not clear. Her argument that his children would not accept her lacks validity. Second and even third marriages were common in the early nineteenth century, and children, in their flexibility, readily adapted to a new parent.

Sarah also gave her desire to be a minister as a reason, and yet she had, in her own congregation, the model of the gentle and feminine Lucretia Mott, a Quaker minister happily and successfully combining her ministry and her marriage to James Mott.

A few years later Israel Morris again proposed. Again Sarah refused him, this time finally and irrevocably. She settled into a pattern of a life of good works within the framework of the Quaker community.

## Angelina

Blue-eyed, blond Angelina Emily Grimké, born on February 20, 1805, quickly became the spoiled darling of the entire household. Under the care and supervision of her godmother, elder sister Sarah, little Nina, as the baby of the family, soon came to expect to have her own way.

Unlike Sarah, who was assailed by self-doubts, Angelina was self-assured and self-confident. Sarah had been crushed by the thwarting of her intellectual ambitions. It never occurred to Angelina that she might be considered inferior simply because she was a girl.

When she was thirteen, she electrified her family and the Episcopal rector by announcing that she could not accept the required pledge in her prayer book, and therefore could not go through the ceremony of confirmation.

At the age of eighteen, she joined the Presbyterian church on the grounds that Presbyterians expounded a more liberal philosophy than Episcopalians. To her disappointment, she was unsuccessful in persuading the young minister to preach from his pulpit his views against slavery which he expressed to her in private conversation. When she realized that the liberalism of Presbyterianism did not include race, she became disillusioned with this denomination as well.

When Sarah returned from Philadelphia for brief visits, she found her younger sister increasingly receptive to Quakerism. Angelina began attending Quaker services, and found that the congregation, never very large, had dwindled to two old men who were not on speaking terms with each other. When Angelina attempted to bring about a reconciliation by lecturing them on Christian kindness, she was requested to mind her own business.

The neighbors began to question the propriety of her behavior in attending services with two old men. Angelina's spirited response was that the doors and windows were wide open, and all were invited to attend.

Like her sister before her, Angelina abhorred slavery. She naively believed that, alone and unaided, she could do something about the slave system. Ultimately, however, she realized that one person was powerless to change a system deeply imbedded in a complex social structure.

In 1829 Angelina decided to join Sarah and Anna in Philadelphia. So open had been her personal struggle that it was evident that her departure was a public protest against slavery.

Mary Smith Grimké gave her blessing to her daughter's decision to move north. She recognized the irreconcilable nature of the differences between Angelina and herself on the slavery issue, and believed that Angelina would be better off in the North. Despite their differences, she loved this youngest child of hers tenderly and mourned the parting with deep sorrow.

Angelina was never to return to the South, and she was never to see her mother again.

In Philadelphia, Angelina followed her sister into the Quaker communion. She organized a Sunday school class for inmates of the Arch Street prison. When her sister Anna opened a school in her home to supplement her inheritance in order to be able to support her daughter, Angelina moved in with her and became a teacher in Anna's school. Like Sarah, Angelina keenly felt her lack of a sound academic education. She grew weary of keeping one lesson ahead of the pupils, and made a trip to Hartford, Connecticut, to take a look at the Female Seminary run by Catherine Beecher, eldest child of the well-known preacher, Lyman Beecher.

Angelina returned to Philadelphia and announced her intention of enrolling in Catherine Beecher's Female Seminary the following fall. She was astonished at the reaction her decision produced. Her Quaker friends feared that she would be unsafe among so many Presbyterians! Her ardent suitor, Edward Bettle, stopped calling on her. Hurt and bewildered, Angelina, who never before in her life had cared what people thought of her actions, yielded to the pressure and abandoned the idea.

However, Edward Bettle did not resume his visits. To his way of thinking, Angelina's mind had been unsettled. Presumably, her mental stability was not to be trusted—ever again. In 1832 Edward Bettle died in a cholera epidemic.

At ages forty-three and thirty, Sarah and Angelina Grimké faced a bleak future. By the standards of the times, with no marital prospects and no vocation, they had nothing to look forward to, nothing to live for.

In reality, the sisters were just beginning.

## Rebels

During their first several years in Philadelphia the sisters, having escaped from the environment of slavery, had been content merely to engage in good works. Because each had learned for herself the hard lesson of the powerlessness of one individual to change the slave system in the South, neither seems to have considered jumping onto the abolitionist bandwagon in the North.

In 1833 the American Anti-Slavery Society was formed. William Lloyd Garrison began publishing *The Liberator,* in which he advocated immediate, as opposed to gradual, emancipation for the slaves. The Grimké sisters became readers of Garrison's publication.

A series of riots in 1834 in New York, Philadelphia, and Concord, Massachusetts, in which both abolitionist leaders and helpless Negroes were attacked by mobs, coincided with a riot in Charleston, South Carolina, in which a mob attempted to destroy a shipment of antislavery literature which had arrived at the post office.

The realization that there was no hiding place from the evils of the slave system which she had fled Charleston to escape apparently weighed heavily upon the mind and heart of Angelina Grimké.

She wrote a personal letter to William Lloyd Garrison, deploring mob violence and affirming the cause of abolition. Without consulting her, Garrison published the letter, stating in a preface that he did so without the writer's knowledge or permission. The effect of the publication of such a letter, under the signature of a member of an old and distinguished Southern family, was electrifying.

The Quakers condemned Angelina for having written the letter and urged her to retract it. Even Sarah strongly disapproved. But for Angelina there was no turning back. From that day forward, the illustrious Southern name of Grimké was irrevocably linked with the Northern cause of abolition.

Barred from active participation in the American Anti-Slavery Society, a group of women, under the leadership of Lucretia Mott, had formed their own organization, the Philadelphia Female Anti-Slavery Society, in 1833. It is not known when the Grimké sisters joined the organization, but by 1835 Angelina had become a member of a committee. Eventually Sarah joined her younger sister in becoming a member of the organization.

In the Society the sisters met Sarah Douglass, a Negro school teacher, and her mother, Grace. Their close friendship endured for many years. This friendship had a profound influence on the sisters' sensitivity to racial prejudice and injustice.

Increasingly restless in her search for something she could do to help the cause of abolition, Angelina wrote an *Appeal to the Christian Women of the South* in the summer of 1836. The document is remarkable in that it is the only appeal to have been written by a Southern abolitionist woman to Southern women.

In the appeal, Angelina assured the women that she was writing them in Christian love, and begged them to accept her appeal in the same spirit. She invoked many arguments, including biblical ones, against slavery. She urged women, who could not vote, to exercise their influence over their husbands, fathers, and brothers, who could. She urged women to petition their state legislatures for the freeing of the slaves. She urged them to read, pray, speak, and act on the subject of slavery.[2]

"Are there no Miriams, who would rejoice to lead out the captive daughters of the Southern States to liberty and light? . . . Is there no

Esther among you who will plead for the poor devoted slave?"[3] she entreated.

The reaction to this impassioned appeal was predictable. In the North the American Anti-Slavery Society heralded it as a valuable contribution to the abolitionist cause, printed it as a pamphlet, and gave it wide distribution. In the South it was berated. Copies were burned publicly by the postmaster in Charleston, South Carolina, and the warning was issued that the author should never dare show her face there.

Angelina received an invitation from the American Anti-Slavery Society to come to New York and speak to women in private parlors on the subject of slavery and abolition.

In the early 1800s it was unthinkable for a woman to give a public lecture. It was acceptable for a woman to address a group of women in parlor talks—small gatherings in private homes. But a woman addressing a mixed audience, termed in the vocabulary of the times a "promiscuous" audience, on a public platform, was nothing short of scandalous.

Up to 1836 only one woman had dared to do so: Frances Wright, an Englishwoman. Fanny, as she was called, gave public lectures to promiscuous audiences on such far-out topics as free thought, public education for all children, equal rights for women, and a ten-hour day for the workingman![4] Because of her unconventional behavior in traveling about unescorted and speaking in public, her personal morals were attacked. An action or occasion to be disparaged was derisively termed "Fanny Wrightism" or a "Fanny Wright affair."

When Angelina decided to accept the New York invitation, which also included her older sister, Sarah pondered her own role in the matter. A letter from her mother in South Carolina decided her. Mrs. Grimké wrote that while she did not agree with Angelina's views on abolition she hoped that Sarah would not permit Angelina to embark upon this venture alone. She entreated Sarah to accompany her younger sister to New York.

And so the Grimké sisters from Charleston, South Carolina, became the first female abolitionist agents in the United States.[5]

The sisters underwent an intensive training course for abolitionist speakers, conducted by several well-known abolitionist leaders, including Theodore Weld, one of the movement's most powerful speakers.

It soon became evident that no private home would be adequate to hold the audience anticipated for Angelina's parlor talks, and it was decided to hold the first meeting in the session room of a Baptist church offered by the pastor. There was some consternation that Angelina's speaking in a church, even to an all-female audience, might be considered Fanny Wrightism. In the end, the decision held.

Angelina delivered her first lecture in the Baptist church, her second in a Presbyterian church. In the latter, the audience was so large that the meeting had to be held in the sanctuary. Angelina Grimké experienced an awesome reaction to the idea of speaking behind a pulpit—something no woman did in the 1830s.

From that time on, the sisters worked as a team. Sarah presented the theological and biblical arguments against salvery. Angelina dealt with the organizational aspects. Angelina's speaking debut in New York City marked the beginning of a speaking tour which took the sisters through New York State and into New Jersey.

In May, 1837, the sisters were invited to give a series of lectures in Massachusetts.

At a meeting sponsored by the Boston Female Society in Washington Hall, Angelina addressed an audience of four hundred women.

Sensing in Massachusetts an atmosphere conducive to openness and new ideas which had been lacking in New York, the sisters publicly proposed a new approach to women's participation in the antislavery movement. They urged women to develop a new self-image which would enable them to view themselves as responsible human beings, with no need for self-effacement in the presence of men.[6]

The phenomenon of refined Southern ladies speaking in public began to draw men as well as women to the sisters' lectures. At a meeting in Lowell attended by one thousand persons, a large number of men were in the audience. Thereafter the sisters' lectures were attended by both men and women. Their lecture series in Odeon Hall in Boston drew audiences numbered in the thousands.[7]

Angelina created another public sensation by addressing a committee of the Massachusetts Legislature—the first woman ever to address a state legislature—on the subject of antislavery petitions.

In 1837 a series of open letters written by Sarah, entitled *Letters on the Equality of the Sexes,* appeared in print. In one of the letters was this eloquent plea:

> But I ask no favors for my sex. I surrender not our claim to equality.

All I ask of our brethren is, that they will take their feet from off our necks and permit us to stand upright on that ground which God designed us to occupy. If he has not given us the rights which have, as I conceive, been wrested from us, we shall soon give evidence of our inferiority, and shrink back into that obscurity, which the high souled magnanimity of man has assigned us as our appropriate sphere.[8]

Their public appearances, together with their writings, catapulted the sisters into the center of a controversy which split the abolition movement. Their detractors berated the sisters as having interjected the secondary concern of women's rights into the major concern of abolition, to the detriment of the more important cause of the two, abolition. Their supporters heralded the sisters as crusaders who had brought the two equally important causes together in one focus, to the mutual benefit of both causes.

Theodore Weld was one of the sisters' strongest supporters, and the sisters were among the noted abolitionist leader's most ardent admirers. First resisting, then acknowledging their strong attraction and affection for each other, Angelina Grimké and Theodore Weld were married in Philadelphia on May 14, 1838.

Two days after the wedding, Angelina addressed a meeting of the Anti-Slavery Convention of American Women in newly constructed Pennsylvania Hall. An angry mob raged outside, and the next day burned the building to the ground.

Angelina's marriage marked the end of the sisters' meteoric public-speaking career. The responsibilities of managing a household and caring for three children, together with the struggle against poverty in which the Welds and Sarah, who made her home with them, were ceaselessly engaged, proved too overwhelming to permit the sisters to continue to be active participants in the antislavery movement.

The Welds and Sarah settled first in Fort Lee, New Jersey. Two years later they purchased a farm in Belleville and operated a boarding school with twenty pupils. For a brief period they were part of a communal settlement called Raritan Bay Union in Perth Amboy.

In 1863 the trio moved to Massachusetts, settling in Hyde Park, south of Boston.

Sarah Grimké died on December 23, 1873, at the age of eighty-one. Angelina Grimké Weld died on October 26, 1879, at age seventy-four. Both sisters died in Hyde Park and were buried in Mount Hope Cemetery in Boston.

## A Model for Today

Sarah Grimké had a martyr complex which she never quite succeeded in overcoming. She never completely recovered from her deep disappointment in being denied the opportunity to study law. As a woman of forty-three in Philadelphia, having reached a point when her life seemed to be without purpose or direction, she experienced a resurgence of the old feelings of resentment at her lack of a sound academic education or of any training for a vocation.

Sarah's refusal of Israel Morris's proposal of marriage appears to have had no other basis then that Sarah was playing the martyr. Her enjoyment of martyrdom, whether conscious or unknown even to herself, surfaced repeatedly in her relationship with Angelina. Sarah's protective attitude toward her younger sister began with Angelina's birth when Sarah became her godmother and continued thereafter, even extending into Angelina's marriage.

Closely aligned to martyrdom was a strong tendency toward self-pity, self-denial, and resignation, which found numerous expressions throughout Sarah's life.

Angelina Grimké in her growing-up years was self-centered and self-willed. Spoiled from infancy by the entire family—through no fault of her own—she learned to expect to have her own way. Upon Judge Grimké's death, the family became a household of women. Angelina soon emerged as the dominant figure in the small, feminine family circle.

She attempted, unsuccessfully, to convert her mother and sisters, together with her brothers when they came home to visit, to her way of thinking about slavery and religion.

The only major disagreement the sisters ever had was a misunderstanding over the care of Angelina's children. When Angelina's health became fragile, Sarah took on the responsibility of the care of the three Weld children. Without ever intending to do so, she usurped her sister's place as the children's mother. The tense situation was ultimately resolved and the sisters were reconciled.

The sisters worked together as a harmonious team. Although Angelina was the main attraction in their lecture appearances, there is no evidence of rivalry or jealousy between the sisters. Angelina, as the more gifted speaker of the two, encouraged her sister in her public-speaking efforts. Sarah was proud of her talented younger sister, and considered her role to be that of supporting Angelina.

Angelina exercised her strong will to resist the pressure to retract her letter to William Lloyd Garrison, the publication of which marked the beginning of her involvement in the movement. Her action undoubtedly influenced her sister in a similar direction.

Sarah was the first of the pair to link the cause of women's rights with the cause of abolition. She was far ahead of other reformers of her time in her concern about working conditions for women and children who worked long hours in factories. In the 1830s there were no laws limiting the length of the working day and no laws protecting children from being compelled to work long hours at a young age. The 1938 federal law which established sixteen as the minimum age for the employment of children was a century in the future. Women school teachers were paid half as much as men. Sarah Grimké was one of the first to advocate equal pay for equal work.

Sarah was deeply concerned about these conditions. She began to draw parallels between the status of slaves and the status of women and to ask the same questions in regard to women that abolitionists had long been asking in regard to slaves—questions concerning the right to freedom and the dignity of personhood.

As the elder sister had followed the younger into espousing the cause of abolition, so the younger followed the elder in supporting the cause of women's rights.

The sisters faced the supreme test of their professed belief in racial equality when they discovered the existence of two mulatto nephews, sons of their brother Henry. Angelina read in the *Anti-Slavery Standard* that a young man named Grimké had delivered an outstanding address at Lincoln University, a school for Negro men in Pennsylvania.

She wrote a letter to the young man in which she introduced herself and asked if he were the former slave of one of her brothers. The young man replied that he, Archibald Henry Grimké, was the son of Henry Grimké of Charleston, South Carolina. His mother, Nancy Weston, had been the slave of Henry Grimké and had borne him three children. The youngest, John, was still in Charleston with his mother. The middle brother, Francis James, was with Archibald at Lincoln University.

The sisters invited the young men to visit them, and, at considerable personal sacrifice, financed their education. Archibald graduated from Harvard Law School, and Francis from Princeton Theological Seminary. Both became outstanding leaders and national figures.

Many abolitionists of the time would have maintained the relationship on the level of polite correspondence. The Grimké sisters lived out their beliefs.

Although the Grimké sisters' public career spanned only a brief three-year period, their role in the movements they espoused was a major one with far-reaching and long-lasting effects.

The sisters were the first to demonstrate that women could be effective public speakers, as acceptable to men as to women.

They influenced such young women as Elizabeth Cady Stanton, Abby Kelley, and Lucy Stone, who were to be future leaders of the women's rights movement.

The outstanding models of the lives of Sarah and Angelina Grimké are deep compassion for human suffering and injustice, dedication to a cause in which they profoundly believed, and personal integrity that motivated them to practice privately the principles they publicly proclaimed.

The Grimké sisters from South Carolina were truly rebels with a cause.

## Questions for Reflection

1. Mary Smith Grimké never embraced the abolitionist views of her daughters, but she continued to keep in close touch with them through letters and she never wavered in her love for them, even treating them in her will exactly the same as her other children. Do you find it difficult to reject an idea or belief without rejecting the person who holds it? Give specific instances when you have succeeded in rejecting the idea while continuing to accept the person.

2. Eliza, another Grimké sister, wrote her sisters in the North about the hunger and privation resulting from the Civil War. She added that she would still be willing to die for slavery and the Confederacy. Sarah and Angelina invited Eliza to come North, and lavished tender, loving care upon her for several years until she chose to return to Charleston. Have you ever tried to "kill" an opponent with kindness? What were the results?

3. The Grimké sisters played a public role that had never before been taken by women and carried it off with aplomb. Have you ever found yourself cast in a role that was unusual for you? How did you handle it?

4. The Grimké sisters put their beliefs into practice in

welcoming their nephews into the family. Can you think of instances in which pronouncements were turned into a sham because actions did not verify the words? Have you ever been guilty of this?

5. What models for today do you see in the lives of Sarah and Angelina Grimké?

# 4

# PILGRIM IN THE PROMISED LAND

*Sojourner Truth*

(c. 1797-1883)

## Isabella

Her name was Isabella, and she was born a slave.

The exact year of her birth is not known because the births of slaves were not recorded, but it is believed to have been around 1797. She was born in Ulster County, New York, in the heart of a Dutch settlement, and because she was owned by a family of that nationality her first language was Dutch. Eventually she passed through the ownership of several families, in the course of which she learned to understand and to speak English.

Isabella's father was named James but was called Baumfree, meaning "straight as a tree." Her mother, Elizabeth, or Betsey, was almost universally called Mau-Mau Bett. Although outwardly as placid and submissive as her husband, Mau-Mau Bett had a mind of her own. She passed on to her daughter the qualities of courage and determination that were to stand her in good stead all her life.

One of Isabella's earliest childhood recollections was her parents' lamentations over their children who had been sold away from them. By the time Bell, as she was called, was old enough to be aware, only she and her younger brother, Peter, were left to their parents. Bell had no memory of her eleven older brothers and sisters. The overriding fear of Mau-Mau Bett's life was that her remaining daughter and son would be sold away from her and she would be left bereft of all her children.

One day Colonel Hardenbergh, the master, died, and the slaves passed into the ownership of the eldest son, Master Charles. The slaves considered themselves fortunate because Master Charles was believed to be the best of the lot. Then he, too, died, and the ominous word was passed around: the slaves were all to be sold at auction.

On the next auction day Isabella and Peter were taken to the slave market and sold to different masters.

At the age of nine Isabella faced the world alone.

Her new master was a small farmer and merchant named John Neely, who had never owned a slave before and had had no intention of buying one that day. The scrawny girl was thrown in for nothing with a flock of sheep Neely purchased, and so he found himself the owner of a slave. Neely decided that the way to keep a slave in line, especially one who did not speak or understand a word of English, was to administer routine beatings. He beat the child Bell upon the slightest pretext.

Mrs. Neely had even less understanding of slaves than her husband, and interpreted Bell's inability to follow instructions given in English as sheer perversity. She contributed many cuffs and bruises to Bell's daily portion of punishments.

It was from Neely that Isabella received the worst beating of her life. She never knew the reason for the whipping. She was simply told by Mrs. Neely to go to the barn. There she found Neely waiting. He ordered her to bare her back and tied her hands together in front of her so that she could not ward off the blows. He beat her until the blood lay in pools at her feet. When the beating was over, the child lay in a state of semiconsciousness on the floor.

Mau-Mau Bett had always taught her daughter that if she would pray to God he would hear her and help her. Through a haze of pain the nine-year-old child wondered why God had not taken care of her. Later, Bell went off by herself and talked to God about the matter. She told him about the beating. "Do you think that's right, God?" she bellowed, thinking that she must shout to make God hear her, away up there in the sky.

One day Bell's father came to see her—the new home was but a short distance from the old. When he left, Bell walked to the gate with him. Out of view of her inquisitive mistress, Bell showed him the deep gashes on her back made by the lashes of Neely's whip. She begged her father to find her a new master.

Baumfree was heartsick and angry at this cruel treatment of his child. Although he had been freed by New York State law, he had no means of livelihood and could not help his daughter directly. But he spread the word around about what a fine worker she was. A prospective buyer went to Neely and offered him $105 in cash for Isabella. Neely quickly accepted the offer, and Isabella had a new master.

Martin Schryver, Bell's new owner, operated several fishing boats and was the proprietor of a tavern and grog shop. He and his wife made scant distinction between master and slave. Skimpily educated, rough and crude, the Schryvers were simple, honest, and kind. Bell thrived on the outdoor life, unloading the fishing boats, hoeing corn, riding horses, helping in the tavern, acquiring a colorful vocabulary, running free. Life was a joyous adventure. The God of Mau-Mau Bett faded into the recesses of Bell's mind.

But the good life was not to be for long.

After about fourteen months of carefree, boisterous living, the tall, sturdy girl caught the eye of a plantation owner named John Dumont from nearby New Paltz, New York. Dumont offered Schryver three times the amount he had paid for Isabella. Schryver hesitated. He and his wife liked Isabella and were loathe to let her go. But their casual way of handling their business affairs kept them financially strapped. They needed the money. Reluctantly, they accepted the offer.

And so Isabella, at the age of thirteen, came to the household of John Dumont, where she was to spend the next seventeen years of her life.

She got along well with Dumont; and because she was a hard worker and had endless energy, she quickly became his favorite slave. Unfortunately, Dumont's partiality for his new acquisition was not shared by his wife. Bell's airy independence annoyed Mrs. Dumont. Whenever Isabella helped Mrs. Dumont in the kitchen, she was forced to endure many scoldings and reprimands from Mrs. Dumont's sharp tongue.

When Bell was sixteen and accounted fully a woman, she met Robert, a young man from a neighboring plantation who was to be the only love of her life. Their marriage was never to be. Robert's master was not about to jeopardize his rights to any future children of his strong, robust slave by permitting him to marry outside his own plantation. He forbade Robert to see Bell again.

But the young man's ardor was not so easily quelled. Hearing that Bell was ill, he went to see her. His master and his master's son followed him, and gave him a beating so vicious that he was dragged away unconscious. Robert later died, as much from a broken spirit, the slaves said, as from the savage blows to his head.

Soon afterward, Bell, at her master's insistence, was married to Thomas, an older slave on the Dumont plantation, and in the course of the next several years bore him four daughters and a son.

A few months after the birth of Bell's first child in 1817, a law was passed to free all the remaining slaves in New York State. Under a previous law, passed in 1799, all slaves born after July 4 of that year were born free but had to remain with their masters as unpaid servants—boys to the age of twenty-eight and girls to the age of twenty-five.

Had Bell been born two years later she would have been born free under the law. But she was born in 1797, two years *before* the law was passed, and so was doomed to a life of slavery until the new law provided the promise of freedom. Under the new law all slave owners had to free all slaves born before July 4, 1799. The owners were given ten years in which to accomplish this. Freedom Day was July 4, 1827.

Because Bell was her master's favorite slave, he promised her that he would give her her freedom a year before the new law made it mandatory. A year before Freedom Day, Bell eagerly waited for Dumont to fulfill his promise to give her her freedom. But when the time came, he changed his mind. After all, he was only breaking his word to a slave.

To her own astonishment, drawing on inner strength and resourcefulness she had not known she possessed, Bell simply took her baby, Sophia, in her arms, and walked away.

It was to be but the first of many walks for this amazing woman.

## Mystic

Isabella did not walk very far.

As a slave whose every move throughout her life had been decided for her by others, she had never learned how to plan. She knew only that she was entitled to her freedom and that to obtain it she must take matters into her own hands.

When she had walked but a short distance, she met a kindly old man who directed her to the home of Isaac and Maria Van Wagener, Quakers morally opposed to slavery. The warm-hearted couple received the runaway mother and child sympathetically.

Dumont came in pursuit of his prize slave, as she had known he would. When Bell refused to return with him, he bargained with the

Van Wageners for possession of her. Bell had served John Dumont for seventeen years. He sold her in thirty seconds for twenty dollars.

Under New York State law, baby Sophia was already free, but Dumont was entitled to her services until she reached the age of twenty-five. Again Dumont bargained with the Van Wageners. The Quaker couple purchased the baby's services from Dumont for five dollars.

Having got what he came for, Dumont departed.

Isabella considered that she now belonged to the Van Wageners, but her new benefactors soon enlightened her. The money they had paid Dumont was not for possession of Isabella and Sophia. It was for their freedom.

Isabella was free at last.

While Isabella was still with Dumont, he had sold the services of her son, Peter. In direct violation of New York State law, the boy had been taken to Alabama to live. Fearful that her son would be doomed to a life of slavery in the South while under New York law he was technically free, Isabella enlisted the help of the Van Wageners and other Quaker friends in securing her son's return to the North.

This unlearned ex-slave, who could neither read nor write, laboriously and persistently unraveled the complicated process of suing in a court of law to get her son returned to her, and won.

Life with the Van Wageners settled into a comfortable routine. Isabella cooked, cleaned, and did the laundry. She ate at the same table with the Quaker couple, who insisted upon being addressed as Isaac and Maria—friends, not masters. Isabella took their last name as her own, and became known as Isabella Van Wagener.

But something within Isabella's restless spirit remained unsatisfied.

Somehow Peter must be given an education. When the opportunity came for Isabella to move to New York City, she said farewell to the Van Wageners, gathered up her son and baby daughter, and went.

The year was 1829. Isabella supported herself and her two children by working as a domestic. She first attended a Methodist church and later a Zion African church.

Through her employer, Isabella met a wealthy merchant named Elijah Pierson and his wife, Sarah. Pierson was an emotionally unbalanced religious fanatic who called himself "The Tishbite." Isabella joined her new friends in preaching on street corners in one of the worst parts of the city in a mission to convert the prostitutes of the area. Eventually she became a member of the Pierson household.

When a bearded charlatan whose name was Robert Matthews but who called himself Matthias appeared, the three naive mystics were ripe for the plucking. They accepted at face value the stranger's claim to have a divine mission to establish a kingdom.

When Isabella ran away from Dumont, she had left her daughters, except for baby Sophia, on the Dumont plantation. Although they were legally free, Dumont was entitled to their services until they should reach the age of twenty-five, and Isabella knew that they would be well cared for by Dumont, who, by the standards of the times, was a kind master. Still, her dream was to have all her children with her, and out of her salary she had set up a fund for the purchase of a small house.

Matthias persuaded her to pour her entire savings, together with the few pieces of furniture she had accumulated, into the communal farm he proposed to establish at Sing Sing, New York—a kingdom to be named Zion Hill. The Piersons also joined in this venture.

The kingdom lasted a brief two years. Pierson died under mysterious circumstances in which death by poisoning was suspected. Although the official investigation cleared Isabella of all suspicion, a member of the community named Benjamin Folger published a book in which he implicated Isabella in the presumed poisoning of Pierson.

A sympathetic newspaperman, Gilbert Vale, published a counterversion of the story, substantiated by character references from every owner and employer Isabella had ever had, including John Dumont.

With Vale's help and encouragement, Isabella sued Folger for libel. Again this illiterate ex-slave entered her case in a court of law and won. The court awarded her $125.

After this disturbing and disillusioning experience, Isabella lived quietly in New York City for nine years. It is not known where her son and daughter were during her residence at Zion Hill. Probably they were cared for by friends or by her older daughters. Upon her return to the city following the collapse of the kingdom, Isabella again had her children with her and supported them and herself by doing housework.

By this time Sophia was seven years old and Peter was in his teens. Always difficult to control, generous, friendly, and well-mannered, Peter fell easy prey to the pitfalls of life in the city. He had several brushes with the law. In desperation, Isabella finally succeeded in persuading her son to sign up as a seaman on a whaling vessel.

Although Isabella could not write, she dictated several letters to Peter. It was evident from his letters to his mother that he never received hers. After his third letter, Isabella never heard from her son again. Presumably he had been lost at sea.

At some point during this period Isabella sent her daughter Sophia to the care of her other daughters, who were still on the Dumont plantation.

Meanwhile, Isabella's restless spirit was asserting itself once more.

She had become increasingly a mystic with the passing years, often hearing voices which guided her actions. On June 1, 1843—she was presumed to be about forty-six years old at this time—she heard her "voices," which she firmly believed to be from the Lord, telling her to "go East."

For the second time in her life, this intrepid woman dropped a change of clothing, a few coins, and some bread and cheese into a pillowcase, bade her employers, the Whitings, good-bye, and simply walked away.

## Sojourner

"East" was Brooklyn.

Clutching the fare in her hand, Isabella boarded the Brooklyn ferry. On the other side, she spent the summer walking through Long Island and Connecticut, sleeping wherever she could find shelter.

As she walked, she was given her new name, as she firmly believed, from the Lord. First she heard her new first name, "Sojourner," because she was to travel up and down the land. As she continued walking, she longed for a last name "with a handle to it." Like a voice from heaven, it came to her: "Sojourner *Truth*" because she was to declare truth unto the people. She was delighted with her new name, and leaped in the air for joy.[1]

And so the former slave who had been named Isabella Van Wagener became Sojourner Truth, and Sojourner Truth she was to remain to the end of her life.

Sojourner—for that was now her name—began preaching, first in the streets and then in camp meetings. She preached her way to

Northampton, Massachusetts, where she happened onto a communal silk farm, which was called the Northampton Association of Education and Industry. Sojourner became laundress for the community. The Association was her home for the next three years, until its collapse in 1846.

Here Sojourner encountered the abolitionist movement for the first time and embraced it enthusiastically. She soon became one of the movement's most effective speakers. Although she could not read, she had a thorough knowledge of the Bible and could quote it extensively in debate. Her pungent knack for piercing the kernel of an issue, together with the primitive English she used to express her ideas, soon earned her a reputation as a picturesque speaker. The abolitionist leaders were quick to recognize her value to the movement, and publicized in their periodicals her speaking forays throughout Massachusetts.[2]

Sojourner had no means by which to support herself. She had lost her life savings in Matthias's kingdom. She had worked in the Northampton silk farm as a member of the community, volunteering her services like everyone else.

A friend, Olive Gilbert, offered to write down Sojourner's autobiography as Sojourner dictated it. After Sojourner paid the printer from the copies she sold, additional sales would become a means of supporting herself.

It was in the year 1850 that Sojourner Truth began to sell her autobiography, which was entitled *The Narrative of Sojourner Truth*. The Anti-Fugitive Slave Bill had just become law, and the abolitionists set out to oppose it. Sojourner's book, the first by an ex-slave who was both a Northerner and a woman, would help the cause.

In a meeting during which abolitionist leader William Lloyd Garrison called her to the platform to say a few words, she was to be followed by Wendell Phillips. She pondered what she could say that would be remembered after such a dynamic speaker as Phillips had spoken. She decided that she must do something Phillips could not do: she would sing a song of her own composition.

To her surprise, after the meeting when people rushed over to buy her book, they wanted her song, too. After that, she sold printed copies of her songs and postcard pictures of herself, which she called her "shadow," along with her book.

Sojourner embarked upon a lecture tour with George Thompson, the English abolitionist. They made their way through

New York State, speaking in the towns along the Erie Canal, coming at last to Rochester. Thompson crossed over into Canada to give a lecture, but Sojourner decided to remain and make some speeches in Rochester, where people were eager to hear an abolitionist speaker.

Here she again met Frederick Douglass, an ex-slave whom she had known during the stay at the Northampton Association in Massachusetts and who had settled in Rochester. He had become the publisher of an antislavery paper called *The North Star,* and headed the local branch of the Underground Railroad, by which runaway slaves were smuggled into Canada.

Since the passage of the Anti-Fugitive Slave Law, runaway slaves were no longer safe even in free-state New York. The law provided that fugitives could be hunted down, even in the free states, and returned to their owners in the South. Furthermore, anyone caught harboring or aiding a slave was subject to a heavy fine.

At her first lecture meeting in Rochester, Sojourner met an unassuming woman named Amy Post, who invited Sojourner to stay with her and her husband, Isaac. The Posts were well known locally as abolitionists and, as Sojourner soon discovered, were active in the operation of the Underground Railroad.

More than once, in the middle of the night, Sojourner was awakened by the clatter of horses' hooves drawing the Post carriage, headed toward the Genesee River and the steamers bound for Canada—and freedom for the fugitives.

Life in Rochester was pleasant, but once again Sojourner grew restless. Eight years earlier, in 1843, a servant named Isabella Van Wagener had heard the voice of the Lord, telling her to "go East." Now, in 1851, that same voice spoke to the abolitionist Sojourner Truth, telling her to "go West."

Bidding the Posts good-bye, she boarded the westward-bound steamer.

## Pilgrim

Her first stop was Akron, Ohio. Sojourner had heard that a women's rights convention was to be held there. She had rightly guessed that she would be the only Negro present. She was given a cool reception because the women feared that her presence would mix up their cause with that of abolition.

Several preachers spoke in the meeting, expounding the innate superiority of the male sex, both physically and mentally. One minister cited Eve, the first sinner, as proof that God had intended to make woman inferior.

Sojourner Truth rose to speak.

But what's all this here talking about? That man over there say that women needs to be helped into carriages, and lifted over ditches, and to have the best place everywhere. Nobody ever helps me into carriages, or over mud puddles, or gives me any best place—and aren't I a woman? . . .

Look at me! Look at my arm! . . . I've plowed and planted and gathered into barns, and no man could head me—and aren't I a woman? I could work as much as a man, and eat as much, when I could get it, and bear the lash as well. And aren't I a woman?[3]

I have borne children and seen them sold into slavery, and when I cried out with a mother's grief, none but Jesus heard me. *And aren't I a woman?* . . .

If the first woman God ever made was strong enough to turn the world upside down all alone, these women together ought to be able to turn it back and get it right-side up again. And now that they are asking to do it, the men better let 'em.[4]

The fickle crowd, which had maintained a hostile silence during the first part of Sojourner's speech, was now delirious in its enthusiasm.

She also attended the Anniversary Convention of the Anti-Slavery Society in Salem, Ohio. Frederick Douglass, in a mood of angry despair, spoke of the thousands of Negro men, women, and children fleeing toward Canada, only to be caught and sent back to the South. The audience was caught up in his contagious mood of pessimism. An aura of futility and despair pervaded the atmosphere.

Slowly Sojourner Truth got to her feet. "Frederick," boomed her deep voice, "is God dead?"

The effect was electrifying. The mood of the audience changed from despair to expectant hope. The God of Sojourner Truth was far from dead!

For the next two years, in a horse and buggy lent her by friends, she traveled through the entire state of Ohio, singing her songs, preaching and speaking wherever she felt called by the Lord to do so, and matching wits with the homespun people of the small towns and rural areas.

After one of her meetings, a man came up to her and said,

"Old woman, do you think that your talk about slavery does any good? Do you suppose people care what you say? Why, . . . I don't care any more for your talk than I do for the bite of a flea." "Perhaps not,

. . ." [Sojourner responded good-naturedly] "but, the Lord willing, I'll keep you scratching."[5]

In 1853, her tour of Ohio completed and the borrowed horse and buggy returned to their owner, Sojourner returned to the East to visit her daughters. But she decided that the East was no longer her home. She felt much more comfortable among the plain-speaking people of the West. In 1856 she decided to settle in Battle Creek, Michigan.

Between her lecture tours she earned her living as she always had—by cooking, cleaning, taking in laundry, and caring for the sick. Among her employers were some of Battle Creek's most illustrious citizens, who were pleased to have her services and who welcomed her to their tables.

From Battle Creek she accompanied her old friend, Parker Pillsbury, the abolitionist, on a lecture tour into Indiana, which proved to be an inhospitable state.

A rumor was circulated that Sojourner Truth in reality was not a woman but a man. While she was waiting to speak, a doctor rose and proposed that Sojourner privately expose her breast to some of the women present so that the question might be resolved, once and for all. The women were embarrassed and angry at such a preposterous proposal.

Sojourner inquired why it was supposed that she might be a man. The response was that her voice was like that of a man.

The doctor called for a vote on the issue, as if in a democracy even the sex of a person could be determined by a majority vote! After the rousing response, the doctor declared that the ayes had carried the proposition, and so Sojourner was voted into the male sex! Sojourner was fully equal to the occasion. She announced that she would show her breast to the entire congregation. As she did so, she declared, "It is not my shame but yours that I should do this."[6]

The years hastened by. Sojourner was getting older, but there was no time to rest. Alone, she traveled in Illinois, Ohio, and Michigan, singing and speaking in behalf of abolition and women's rights wherever she could find an audience.

War clouds hung low over the nation. In 1864 Sojourner decided, with her favorite grandson, Sammy Banks, as her escort, to call upon President Lincoln in the White House.

On the long journey to Washington, Sojourner visited many friends along the way. A previous visit with Harriet Beecher Stowe and the account of the visit by the well-known author published in *The Atlantic Monthly* had increased the scope of Sojourner's fame. As a result, she received so many invitations to speak that her arrival in Washington was greatly delayed.

When she finally gained an audience with the president, she confided to him that she had never heard of him until he ran for president. Lincoln responded that he had heard of her many years before he ever thought of running for president, so well known was she throughout the Middle West.

## Counselor

Sojourner Truth accepted an official commission from the National Freedman's Relief Association as counselor to the freed people in the model village for Negro refugees from the South at Arlington Heights, Virginia. Her job was to instruct the women in housekeeping skills.

Her booming voice soon became a familiar sound resounding through the streets of the village with the ringing exhortation, "Be clean! Be clean! For cleanliness is godliness!"[7] The response of the women was enthusiastic. In no time at all results of Sojourner's teaching were visible. Bedding was aired daily, floors were swept clean, and freshly-scrubbed children were dressed in clean, neatly mended clothing.

A hospital for Negroes had been established, and Sojourner was asked to leave Freedman's Village to give the same kind of help at Freedman's Hospital. Her exhortation to "be clean! be clean!" soon was resounding through the hospital corridors just as it had through the streets of the village. She instructed the nurses in cleanliness and the care of the sick. On Sundays she held services in which she sang old, familiar hymns and her own songs and preached sermons.

In her work at the hospital Sojourner was dependent upon streetcars for transportation. Even though the law forbade segregation in the streetcars, the law was seldom enforced. The conductors either refused to let Sojourner ride at all or insisted upon her standing on the front platform behind the horses. With her customary dignity and flash of spirit, Sojourner exercised her right to ride as a human being.

One conductor gave her a vicious shove which dislocated her shoulder, causing her much pain. Through a lawyer provided by the Freedman's Bureau, Sojourner sued the street railway for assault and battery, and for the third time in her life won her case. The conductor was fired. Thereafter the law was enforced, and Negro passengers were treated with the utmost courtesy.

Following the assassination of Lincoln, Sojourner conceived her idea for a Negro state in the West. Why should not the government give the freedmen some of the vast lands in the West for farming? It would be more economical than the present system of providing refugee camps for the Negroes.

At age seventy-three, Sojourner Truth set out upon the last great mission of her life.

Sojourner traveled many miles—from Philadelphia to Missouri—and collected several thousand signatures on her petitions to present to Congress. But she learned of the utter indifference of Congress to the plight of the Negroes.

Sojourner Truth never returned to Washington. She sadly accepted the hard fact that Congress was not interested in settling the Negroes in the West.

In December, 1877, a remarkable phenomenon occurred. Great numbers of freedmen from the South began migrating to Kansas. By the end of 1879, sixty thousand freedmen had made the long trip northward and westward. In the great migration, Sojourner saw the hand of the Lord, achieving what she alone, in her human frailty, had been unable to accomplish.

Sojourner Truth was an old woman now. As she had not feared life, neither did she fear the approach of death. Many years before, a friend had asked her what she would do if there should turn out to be no heaven and consequently she never got there. Sojourner's response was typical: "Why, I'll say, 'Bless the Lord! I had a good time thinking I would.'"[8]

Sojourner Truth died at her home in Battle Creek on November 26, 1883. Her funeral was said to have been the largest ever held in the town. Nearly a thousand people crowded into the Congregational and Presbyterian Church.[9]

Her tombstone in Oak Hill Cemetery bears this inscription:

Born a Slave in Ulster County,
State of New York, in 18th Century.
Died in Battle Creek, Michigan,
November 26, 1883. Aged about 105 Years.
**"IS GOD DEAD?"** [10]

## A Model for Today

The life of Sojourner Truth is so shrouded in legend that it is difficult to separate fact from fantasy. Her admirers encouraged the legend. Confusing her with her mother, they insisted that she had had thirteen children and two husbands sold away from her. They claimed that she was 105 years of age at the time of her death and not 86. During her lifetime Sojourner Truth herself believed that she was about twenty years older than she actually was.

As a public figure, she possessed a personal magnetism—today it would be called charisma—which, combined with her ready wit and gift for the quick retort, attracted large crowds to hear her speak. When she went West in the early 1850s, she found that her growing reputation as a speaker had preceded her. She became as well known in the Middle West as she was in the East.

Although her role in the movements of the day was a relatively minor one, she achieved such fame that she became a legend in her own lifetime.

Sojourner Truth embodied in her makeup an extraordinary combination of naiveté and practical common sense. As a child, she had believed John Dumont to be God. As an adult in New York City, she had been taken in by the fraudulent claims of Robert Matthews. But after her painful discovery that John Dumont was, after all, a mortal and Robert Matthews was a fraud, she never again considered any human being to have a greater power to know the truth than she herself had. That realization constituted a second Freedom Day for her.[11]

When Sojourner Truth boarded the Brooklyn Ferry that June morning in 1843, she firmly believed herself to be God's emissary, commissioned to carry his message to sinful humanity. For more than forty years not once did she ever serve from that profound conviction.

She constantly listened for the voice of her Lord, telling her where he wanted her to go and what he wanted her to do.

Because she believed that she had a divine commission, she accepted at face value the scriptural injunction to "take no thought for the morrow." She believed, simply and confidently, that God would provide for her daily needs.

The outstanding model presented by the life of Sojourner Truth is that of a free spirit—free in body, free in soul. Unfettered by the bonds of conventionality or appropriateness, she was free to be her own person, to do her own thing. She was mystic, wanderer, pilgrim in the Promised Land.

Truly Sojourner Truth was free at last!

## Questions for Reflection

1. Sojourner Truth gave more time and attention to her religious activities than to her son, and Peter suffered serious consequences from his mother's neglect. Have you found yourself so consumed by your volunteer activities that you had no time for your family or your friends? How did you go about rearranging your priorities?

2. Sojourner Truth, although illiterate and uneducated, possessed a practical common sense and an innate wisdom not to be acquired through a formal education. Name some persons you have known who possessed this kind of wisdom. In what ways did they make use of it?

3. By the standards of today Isabella, the slave mother, would be considered to have deserted her children. In actuality, this was not the case. Can you draw any parallels to the dangers of judging the actions of others on the basis of imposing our own standards upon the situation? Give examples.

4. Sojourner Truth won her freedom by assuming control over her own destiny when John Dumont broke his promise to her to give her her freedom a year early. Can you think of times when you had to take control of the direction of your life? Describe the situation.

5. What models for today do you see in the life of Sojourner Truth?

# 5

# HUMANITARIAN WITH A HEART

*Dorothea Dix*

*(1802-1887)*

## Supplicant

On a blustery March day in 1841 Dorothea Dix taught a Sunday school class for women inmates of the East Cambridge, Massachusetts, jail. That insignificant incident instilled in her a singleness of purpose which was to be the motivating force of her life for the next forty-five years.

Singleness of purpose had characterized Dorothea Dix from early childhood. Born on April 4, 1802, the eldest child and only daughter of her parents, she was given increasing responsibility for the care of her two younger brothers, Joseph and Charles Wesley.

Her mother became a semi-invalid after the birth of her third child. Her father, Joseph Dix, was an itinerant Methodist evangelist who was perpetually on the losing side of the struggle to support his family.

Joseph Dix was the third son of Elijah Dix, a prominent physician, merchant, and real estate investor of Boston, and Dorothy Lynde Dix, the eighth of seventeen children of a distinguished Massachusetts family. Because of a ban on married students, Joseph had been compelled to drop out of Harvard when he married. His wife, Mary Bigelow, was considered by the Dix family to be uneducated and uncouth, totally unworthy to bear the proud name of Dix.

To provide a livelihood for his son and possibly to remove his undesirable daugher-in-law from view, Dr. Elijah Dix made Joseph his agent for his real estate holdings in the village of Hamden—

population, 150—near Bangor. At that time this section of Maine was the rugged frontier of Massachusetts.

At some unknown time, probably when Dorothea was ten, the family left Maine and settled in Worcester, Massachusetts. The family may have been among the refugees created by the War of 1812.

Joseph quickly displayed his ineptitude for the management of business affairs and drifted into preaching. He had always been something of a religious fanatic and soon acquired a reputation as a forceful preacher. The acclaim was good, but the pay was poor, and the family was constantly destitute.

To supplement the family finances, Joseph printed his sermons and sold them as tracts. To keep printing costs to a minimum, Joseph had the printer only set type, and put his wife and daughter to cutting and stitching the pamphlets, a task which young Dorothea passionately hated.

Discouraged by the ceaseless bout with poverty, Joseph gradually slipped back into the intemperate habits of his youth. With a dissolute father and a shiftless mother, Dorothea Dix experienced a childhood so unhappy and so devoid of emotional security that throughout her life she was never to speak of her parents or her childhood years, even to her closest friends.

The blue-eyed little girl had always been a favorite of her grandparents. On her visits to their home in Orange Court in Boston, the doctor always had time for her and often took her with him in his carriage as he made the round of calls on his patients. Although her Grandfather Dix died in 1809, when Dorothea was seven, the little girl never forgot those visits and the personal attention she received from him.

Grandmother Dix was an impeccable housekeeper. The red brick mansion, with its elegant furnishings of thick carpets, fine furniture, draperies, china, and silver, together with the well-ordered routine of the household, provided a sharp contrast to the poverty-ridden, slovenly kept house of Joseph and Mary Bigelow Dix. The little girl found it hard to return home after the visits to Orange Court.

By the time Dorothea was twelve, she realized that her only hope for an education lay with her Grandmother Dix. It is not known how she managed to get from Worcester to Boston, whether her parents arranged transportation for her or whether on her own initiative she secured a ride with a family friend who was traveling by stage to the city. By whatever method she managed the arrangements, one day in 1814 the twelve-year-old child appeared at the Dix family mansion in Orange Court and begged her grandmother's permission to stay.

Grandmother Dix had never liked her daughter-in-law and had never accepted her into the family. She believed that her granddaughter would be better off in her care. Madam Dix informed her son and daughter-in-law that henceforth Dorothea would live with her.

## Teacher

If Dorothea had been unhappy in her parents' ill-kept house, she soon found that she was miserable in the well-ordered, disciplined routine of her grandmother's household. The strong-willed sixty-eight-year-old grandmother soon was engaged in a formidable clash of wills with her equally strong-willed namesake. After two years of trying to handle her headstrong granddaughter, Madam Dix sent her back to Worcester, this time to the care of her sister, Sarah Lynde Duncan, and her sister's daughter, Sarah Duncan Fiske.

Dorothea felt an immediate affinity with the two Sarahs, especially the younger one. Although she was only fourteen, she persuaded her two relatives to permit her to open a school for small children. Soon some of the best families of Worcester were sending their young children to Dorothea's school.

To compensate for her extreme youth, Dorothea lengthened her skirts and adopted the hairstyle of a grown woman. She became a stern disciplinarian and unhesitatingly administered birch-rod punishment to small boys. Little girls were chastened by more subtle kinds of punishment, one of which consisted of being compelled to walk through the streets with a placard on the back proclaiming, "A very bad girl, indeed."[1]

Dorothea was especially strict with her own brother, Joseph, so that she could not be accused of favoritism. She kept her school for almost three years.

In addition to the maturing effect of running her own school, another benefit of life in Worcester was the social contact with her grandmother's many relatives, including cousins Dorothea's own age. Edward Bangs, a second cousin fourteen years older than Dorothea, became the only love of her life.

When Dorothea was seventeen, she returned to her grandmother's home in Boston. She had left as a headstrong, willful child. She returned a poised young woman, with the gracious bearing and charm of manner for which the first Dorothy Lynde Dix, her grandmother, had been noted.

Dorothea spent the next two years completing her own education and preparing herself to be a teacher. Madam Dix was proud of her talented granddaughter and gave her the best education available to girls, first in the public schools and then through private instruction. Dorothea was interested in history, science, and literature, and read profusely on her own.

In 1821 she sought her grandmother's permission to open her own dame school for sons and daughters of well-to-do families. Madam Dix considered it quite unnecessary for the granddaughter of Elijah Dix to support herself by teaching school. While the Dix fortune had been greatly reduced by the dissipations of the Dix sons, including Joseph, it was still sufficient to provide a life of ease for both Madam Dix and her granddaughter.

But the granddaughter's will, while greatly modulated in expression from that of the willful twelve-year-old child of seven years before, was still strong, and in the end the determined young woman prevailed over her grandmother. Dorothea opened her school in the red brick mansion in Orange Court.

The dame schools of the post-revolutionary years were private schools operated by women for both boys and girls from the age of four until they entered the public grammar schools at the age of seven. By Massachusetts state law pupils were required to know how to read before entering public school. The dame schools taught children how to read, along with other subjects. Many parents kept their children in the dame school beyond the age of seven because of the tyrannical disciplinary methods of the public schools.

Dorothea Dix was a born teacher. Although always a strict disciplinarian, she delighted in helping the minds of her pupils to unfold and develop. She rose at dawn in order to make the most of her time in preparation for her classes and in her own study and writing. In the evenings she worked far into the night. Many letters to friends were dated after midnight.

She wrote a textbook for children entitled *Conversations on Common Things,* which was published in 1824. Forty-five years later it had gone through sixty printings. She wrote poetry, some of which was published in literary magazines.

Shortly after she opened her school for affluent children,

Dorothea became greatly concerned about children whose parents could not afford the tuition of a private school. With great ingenuity and finesse, she persuaded her grandmother to permit her to convert the upper room of the carriage house into a classroom for these deprived children.

In addition to the management of her schools, Dorothea also undertook the management of the Dix household. Her grandmother and Madam Dix's daughter, Dorothea's Aunt Mary Dix Harris, both of whom had disapproved of Dorothea's school, soon became proud of her managerial abilities.

Dorothea maintained her friendship with her cousin, Edward Bangs. The pair exchanged numerous letters. Edward Bangs made many visits to Boston and Dorothea visited Worcester occasionally. They became engaged. But for reasons unknown the engagement was broken. The disillusionment of blighted romance came hard to the twenty-four-year-old teacher. She was never to speak of it, even to her most intimate friend, Ann Heath, with whom she maintained a steady correspondence spanning fifty years.

Thenceforth Dorothea closed her mind and heart to romance. She rejected the overtures of prospective suitors. Dorothea Dix never again was receptive to the beckonings of romantic love.

Meanwhile, the rigorous work schedule she had imposed upon herself had taken its toll upon her health. Her doctor insisted that she must give up her teaching for a few years in order to ward off the onslaught of tuberculosis.

For the next few years Dorothea Dix spent most of her time in writing. In 1825 she compiled *Hymns for Children,* some of which were believed to be of her own composition. Like her previous book, this volume, too, was a success. In 1828 she published a collection of ten stories for children entitled *American Moral Tales for Young Persons* and a book of devotional meditations called *Meditations for Private Hours.* In 1829 she published two books, *Garland of Flora* and *The Pearl or Affection's Gift.* Her literary works were typical of the sentimental era in which she lived and have long since been forgotten.[2]

By this time, Dorothea Dix, always religiously sensitive, had become attracted to Unitarianism, so different from the Methodist teachings of her father's faith. She had long been an admirer of Unitarian leader William Ellery Channing. Through mutual friends she became personally acquainted with him and became tutor to his children. A winter spent in the semitropical climate of the Virgin Islands with the Channing family helped to restore Dorothea to health.

In 1831 she opened a new school, this time a combination day and boarding school for girls. Like the old one, the new school was a success. But the responsibilities of a matron of a girls' school were taxing. For five years Dorothea ran her school by sheer force of will.

In the spring of 1836 she suffered a complete nervous and physical collapse, and the school in the red brick mansion in Orange Court was closed forever.

## Advocate

Dorothea sailed for England with friends. The plan was that she would stop for a few months in England and then rejoin her friends in Italy. She became ill in Liverpool. When William Rathbone, a Unitarian of Liverpool, learned that a friend of William Ellery Channing was ill in a Liverpool hotel, he insisted upon removing her to the Rathbone country estate, Greenbank, outside the city.

There Dorothea was given loving care as a member of the family. She was to remain in the Rathbone household for eighteen months. While recuperating with the Rathbones, Dorothea received the news that her mother had died at the age of seventy-six. Although Dorothea appears to have felt scant affection for her mother, she had contributed to her support from her earnings as a teacher. Her father had died fifteen years earlier in 1821.

William Rathbone was a prosperous merchant and philanthropist who was greatly concerned about urban reform. He was deeply involved in alleviating the poverty and poor housing conditions of the Liverpool slums. Many outstanding English statesmen, physicians, and lawyers were frequent visitors at Greenbank and shared their ideas. Dorothea Dix told about her charity school over the carriage house of the Dix mansion.

It was probably at this time that her interest in the plight of the mentally ill was first aroused. So stimulating were these conversations to her intellectually keen mind that forever after she was to refer to her stay with the Rathbones as the jubilee year of her life.

When Dorothea had been a guest at Greenbank for about a year, Madam Dix began to worry that her granddaughter might be overstaying her welcome. Madam Dix was not well and wanted to see her granddaughter again. She wrote and asked "Dolly" to come home. But Dorothea was not able to travel. In April, 1837, Grandmother Dix died.

Now there was no need to hurry back to America. Dorothea remained with the Rathbones until she was fully recovered from her illness. In the fall of 1837 she sailed for home.

Dorothea Dix now confronted a crisis in her life. As the principal heir of her grandmother's estate, together with her inheritance from her grandfather and her own earnings from her teaching, Dorothea was financially independent. But economic security was not enough to satisfy a person of Dorothea's high intelligence. Her fragile health precluded her return to teaching. The idea of a woman in business or the professions, except for teaching, was many years from acceptance by society.

Dorothea's lifelong friend, Ann Heath, also unmarried, was in a similar situation. But Ann was surrounded by her married sisters and brother and a flock of affectionate nieces and nephews. Dorothea had no close family ties. Her brothers were grown. Joseph was in business, and Charles had gone to sea. Her cousins considered that she could have come home to be with her grandmother in her final illness if she had really wanted to do so, and because she hadn't, they treated her coldly.

With the disposal of her grandmother's estate, including the sale of the red brick mansion, Dorothea had no home of her own. She felt disoriented. She was thirty-six and had no clear sense of direction for her life.

When John T. G. Nichols, a Harvard divinity student, solicited her help in securing a woman to teach a Sunday school class for women inmates of the East Cambridge jail, Dorothea informed the young man that she would take on the class herself. The project appealed to her humanitarian impulses. She could have had no inkling of the extent to which that simple decision was to change the course of her life.

Following the class that first Sunday, Dorothea Dix toured the jail. To her horrified astonishment, she found many women whose only crime against society was that of mental illness. These unfortunates were incarcerated with hardened criminals simply because there was no other place to put them. Clad only in flimsy garments, they shivered in the damp, penetrating cold of the raw March day. The jailer informed Dorothea, in response to her questions, that a fire would be unsafe. Moreover, he assured her, insane persons were insensitive to the cold.

Dorothea was incensed. She did not believe that these shivering women could not feel the cold. She did not believe that it was morally right for them to be jailed like criminals. She did not believe that society should any longer be permitted to ignore its responsibility for the mentally ill.

It was true that some efforts already had been made in behalf of the mentally ill. There were several hospitals of the highest caliber, but the number was wholly inadequate to meet the need.

Dorothea continued to teach her Sunday school class at the jail. She continued to implore the jailer to provide heat in the section of the jail which housed the mentally ill. The jailer continued to refuse.

The East Cambridge court was in session. Dorothea had her case presented before the court and won. Thereafter, heat was provided for the quarters of the mentally ill.

Dorothea thought of all the other mentally ill persons in the entire state of Massachusetts, with no one to champion their cause. She consulted with knowledgeable reformers of her acquaintance. They pointed out the numerous obstacles to such a formidable project as the one she was contemplating. There was no agency in Massachusetts with a budget adequate to finance a survey of every facility for the mentally ill in the state.

Dorothea Dix consulted her old friend and mentor, William Ellery Channing, who encouraged her in the project. She thought long and hard and made up her mind. She would finance the enterprise from her personal resources, without the backing or support of any agency, and she personally would make the survey.

From the Channing home she began her tremendous undertaking. Because there were few railroads in Massachusetts at that time, she was compelled to travel by stage to reach many of the places she needed to visit. Long hours of jolting over bumpy roads and of sitting up late at night in lonely inns between connections on the stage became the pattern of her life. After more than one experience in which the carriage broke down and the driver had no tools with which to make repairs, the resourceful traveler began carrying in her handbag simple tools with which to meet such emergencies.

By the end of two years, Dorothea Dix had visited every prison, poorhouse, hospital, private home, and other facility which housed mentally ill persons in Massachusetts. There was scarcely a mentally ill individual in the state whom she had not seen personally.

In her investigation, Dorothea Dix came upon scenes that haunted her for days.

She found a young woman, whose only clothing consisted of inadequate fragments of blanket, shackled by an iron band around her waist anchored to the wall by a chain.

She found a young girl, the daughter of a farmer and his wife, who had become insane. She was kept at the state asylum as long as her father could pay the fee. When he was no longer able to pay, the girl was auctioned off to the care of a family, a common practice. She was kept in the barn, the door to which was always unlocked, affording access at will to the men and boys of the town.

She found a woman who had been confined for years in a cellar. She described her as

> . . . a female apparently wasted to a skeleton, partially wrapped in blankets, furnished for the narrow bed on which she was sitting; her countenance furrowed, not by age, but suffering, was the image of distress; in that contracted space, unlighted, unventilated, she poured forth the wailings of despair: mournfully she extended her arms and appealed to me. . . . When the good Lord shall require an account of our stewardship, what shall all and each answer? [3]

The vision of these sad-faced individuals became an overpowering force which drove Dorothea Dix relentlessly. The same singleness of purpose which had driven her at the age of twelve to secure a home with her Grandmother Dix and at the age of nineteen to win her grandmother's reluctant permission to open her school in Orange Court now found expression in her unshakable determination to be an advocate of the improvident mentally ill.

In January, 1843, she presented a memorial—a detailed report with recommendations—to the legislature of Massachusetts, the first of many memorials she was to present to state legislatures in the years to follow.

That first memorial read, in part:

> I come to present the strong claims of suffering humanity. I come to place before the legislature of Massachusetts the condition of the miserable, the desolate, the outcast. I come as an advocate of helpless, forgotten, insane and idiotic men and women; of beings, sunk to a condition from which the most unconcerned would start with real horror; of beings wretched in our Prisons, and more wretched in our Alms-Houses. . . .

I proceed, Gentlemen, briefly to call your attention to the *present* state of Insane Persons confined within this Commonwealth, in *cages, closets, cellars, stalls, pens! Chained, naked, beaten with rods,* and *lashed* into obedience![4]

After much violent opposition and personal malignment of Dorothea Dix by the press, the Massachusetts legislature accepted her memorial and adopted her proposal for the expansion of the asylum for the mentally ill at Worcester.

New York was the next state Dorothea Dix surveyed. She presented her memorial to the state legislature in 1844. Her recommendation, as in Massachusetts, was for the expansion of the existing facility, and was accepted.

New Jersey had no asylum for the insane. Dorothea Dix's survey revealed appalling conditions. In New Jersey, as in Massachusetts, she was viciously maligned. Finally, the proposal in her memorial was accepted, and authorization was given for the establishment of the New Jersey Insane Asylum at Trenton.

Next came surveys culminating in memorials presented to the state legislatures of Pennsylvania, Kentucky, Tennessee, North Carolina, Mississippi, and Maryland. By 1845 she had traveled sixty thousand miles and visited nine thousand facilities for the improvident mentally ill in all parts of the country.

In 1845 she conceived her idea for a federal grant of five million acres of land to be devoted to facilities for the care of the mentally ill. The proposal was eventually increased to ten million acres. Dorothea lobbied long and hard in Washington. After several defeats, her proposal passed both houses of Congress. Victory seemed assured when in a surprise move President Franklin Pierce vetoed the bill in 1848. Congress failed to override the presidential veto.

Stunned, disillusioned, and exhausted, Dorothea Dix sailed for Europe and a vacation.

## Humanitarian

Her first stop was Greenbank, near Liverpool, England, the hospitable home of the Rathbones where many years before she had spent the jubilee year of her life. There she renewed acquaintance with some of the reformers and statesmen she had met on her previous visit. They told her about the progress that had been effected in conditions for the mentally ill. She told them about her work in America.

Dorothea Dix had come to Europe solely for a vacation. She had no intention of becoming involved in philanthropic or humanitarian enterprises. But the inevitable happened. On a visit to Scotland she discovered deplorable conditions for the mentally ill. She found the Lord Provost lukewarm to the idea of an investigation and correctly suspected that he was about to go to London to take steps to block an investigation. While the Lord Provost leisurely packed his bag preparatory to taking the train the next morning, she boarded the night train for London.

Dorothea secured an interview with the Home Secretary in Downing Street before the Lord Provost could get to him. The investigation was secured, and conditions for the mentally ill of Scotland were vastly improved.

Dorothea moved on to Italy. In response to Ann Heath's suggestion that she inspect the facilities for the mentally ill of Italy, she emphatically declared that no good purpose would be served by subjecting herself to that kind of ordeal. She is next seen conducting such an investigation!

So appalling were the conditions she uncovered in Rome in the very shadow of the Vatican that she secured an audience with Pope Pius to tell him about them. The pope was horrified that such conditions existed and expressed his deep gratitude to Dorothea Dix for bringing them to his attention.

Next came Greece, Turkey, Russia, Sweden, Belgium, and on and on: the European vacation became a two-year crusade in behalf of the mentally ill of fourteen countries.

After returning to America, Dorothea Dix, fifty-four and smiling at the suggestion of friends that she retire, resumed her inspection of facilities for the mentally ill.

Then came the Civil War. Acting characteristically, she appeared in Washington and offered her services and those of a small contingent of women as volunteer nurses. She received a commission from the War Department as superintendent of nurses. Although she had had no hospital or nursing experience, she had acquired, through her years of work with the mentally ill, much expertise in principles and techniques of administration which were easily transferable to hospital administration.

Throughout the years of the war she worked unstintingly, never taking a day off except for one brief period of illness. Even then she issued directions from her sickbed.

Louisa May Alcott, whose service as an army nurse was cut short after six weeks by an attack of pneumonia, wrote affectionately of her superior as a dear old lady, but added that she was also very queer and arbitrary.

Dorothea Dix's exacting standards and rigid requirements often brought her into conflict with military medical personnel. In the end, her adversaries triumphed with the issuance of General Orders 351, which virtually abolished the office of superintendent of nurses. This was a severe blow to Dorothea Dix.

When Secretary of War Stanton asked her to name some item the government could give her as an expression of appreciation for her services, she promptly replied, "The flag of my country." She was overwhelmed when she was presented with the colors on a standard. She bequeathed them to Harvard as an indication of her abiding affection for the school which her father had attended and which had been the intellectual and cultural center of her life as a young woman in Boston.

Dorothea Dix was now sixty-five. Even yet retirement was not for her. Even though her great work lay in the past, she spent the next fifteen years touring and inspecting the mental institutions she had been instrumental in establishing.

At last, at the age of eighty, she appeared at the door of the New Jersey State Insane Asylum at Trenton. She always considered the institutions she was instrumental in bringing into being as her "children." The asylum at Trenton was her first "child," and this first "child" became her last home. The trustees voted unanimously to offer her a home under its roof as its honored and revered guest for the remainder of her life. Although she had the financial means to live in a private rest home, she gratefully accepted the offer to spend her last years in this environment of loving care.

By this time many longtime friends had died: William Ellery Channing, William Rathbone, her brother Joseph, and her friend of fifty years, Ann Heath. But many others remained to give her comfort and support.

Dorothea Dix died on July 18, 1887, at the age of eighty-five.

Charles H. Nichols, a friend and close associate of many years, wrote her English friends of her last illness, death, and burial: "Thus has died and been laid to rest in the most quiet, unostentatious way the most useful and remarkable woman America has yet produced."[5]

The marble marker erected by fellow humanitarian Horace Lamb bears no epitaph, not even the dates of her birth and death, but only the simple inscription:

DOROTHEA L. DIX

It is an inscription that Dorothea Lynde Dix herself might have chosen.

## A Model for Today

Dorothea Dix, in her worst light, was rigid, inflexible, stubborn, and religiously prejudiced. Her Civil War service as superintendent of nurses brought forth her least desirable qualities. She was exacting in her requirements for nurses, refusing to accept any women who did not meet her rigid standards and qualifications. She refused to accept Roman Catholic nuns or members of any religious order, reflecting her personal bias.

In her zeal to eliminate romantic young women or adventure seekers, she banned women under thirty and required all applicants to dress plainly in black or brown dresses—the fashionable hoop skirts of the day were not permitted—and to wear only the simplest hairstyles.

She considered that not only did she have the authority to make final decisions regarding the hiring of nurses but also to make the rules governing their hospital service. Her authoritarian manner brought her into conflict with more than one army physician. Long years of combating the deplorable conditions she found in facilities for the mentally ill had developed in her an arbitrary manner that carried over into other aspects of her life.

She herself was to say in later years that her service as superintendent of nurses was not the work by which she wished her life to be judged.

Dorothea Dix was never able completely to overcome the tendency toward self-centeredness that she acquired during the first four years of her life prior to the birth of her brother Joseph. An eager, loving little girl, deprived of the demonstrative affection she craved, first by her parents and then by her grandmother, she concluded that she was unloved.

To the end of her life she was unable to overcome completely this orphan complex which made it impossible for her ever fully to believe herself loved. In an attempt to compensate for this tendency, which she herself recognized, she drove herself and gave of her means unstintingly and excessively.

But in the life and character of Dorothea Dix the good far outweighed the undesirable. In spite of her unhappy childhood, she had a strong sense of family. When she appeared on the doorstep of the Dix mansion, she was seeking a better life not only for herself but also for her brothers. Within a few years the boys were brought to Orange Court and given a home and an education by their Grandmother Dix.

Charles died at sea in 1843, but Dorothea remained close to Joseph and his wife and often rested in their home.

Dorothea's sense of family found expression in her love for children implemented through her teaching. Her compassion for the underprivileged first found expression in her charity school in the carriage-house loft in Orange Court.

Her sense of compassion deepened and expanded with her widening contact with the suffering and ill treatment of unfortunate persons she encountered in her travels. Quietly and unobtrusively, she dispatched boxes of clothing and other necessities wherever she found need. By the time of her death, she had a long list of persons dependent upon her for financial assistance.

For fifty years Dorothea Dix had no home of her own and keenly felt the lack. Most of the time she lodged in inns and boardinghouses. Visits in the homes of friends often accentuated rather than alleviated her loneliness. In the nineteenth century there was no accepted place in society for a woman alone.

She did not hesitate to deviate from the popular definition of a woman's place. She was well aware that society frowned upon the idea of a woman traveling about the country alone, and yet her travels took her from Massachusetts to Texas, from Oregon to Florida. She was always circumspect in her behavior lest she harm her efforts in behalf of the mentally ill, but she refused to curtail her sphere of influence by limiting her conduct to that proscribed by society.

Dorothea Dix had a deep religious faith. She believed that her efforts in behalf of the indigent mentally ill constituted a God-given mission. Her faith sustained her when her efforts were opposed and even thwarted by her adversaries.

Dorothea Dix was a woman of indomitable personal courage. Her broken engagement to Edward Bangs shattered her romantic illusions but did not embitter her. On the contrary, the experience seems to have enriched her character. President Franklin Pierce's veto of her ten-million-acre bill for the mentally ill was a bitter disappointment to her. General Orders 351, which for all practical purposes abolished the office of superintendent of nurses, was a severe blow. Yet she refused to be defeated by these three major disappointments of her life.

Constancy in friendship, coupled with depth of relationship, was a strong characteristic of her makeup. She maintained a special friendship with Ann Heath for fifty years. William Rathbone, Horace Lamb, William Ellery Channing, and John Greenleaf Whittier were her friends and colleagues for many years.

Singleness of purpose was the motivating force of Dorothea Dix's life. Upon her complete nervous and physical collapse in 1836, which resulted in the closing of her school, her doctor informed her that her fragile health would prohibit her ever being able to teach again. Yet for the next forty-five years she maintained a travel and work schedule calculated to exhaust the most robust constitution. So completely did she lose herself in her mission that consideration for her own physical well-being was completely submerged.

The outstanding model of the life of Dorothy Dix is that of a woman alone who, without the protection and support of a man, considered essential for a woman in the nineteenth century, evolved a life-style that was rich and rewarding to herself and a blessing to all humanity.

## Questions for Reflection

1. Dorothea Dix's grandmother played a crucial role in her granddaughter's growth and development. In our highly mobile society grandchildren and grandparents often live many miles apart and see each other only occasionally. What alternatives do you see to the traditional grandparent-grandchild relationship?

2. Deep friendships of many years' duration characterized the relationships of Dorothea Dix. In twentieth-century society friendships are often transitory and superficial. What solutions can you propose to remedy this situation?

3. Dorothea Dix dauntlessly defied convention in assuming roles not considered appropriate for women of her day, such as traveling alone and engaging in work not considered suitable for a woman. Yet she was not in sympathy with the women's rights

movement. Do you see any discrepancy between her life-style and her attitude toward women's rights? Why or why not?

4. Singleness of purpose was a driving force in the makeup of Dorothea Dix. Name some other persons from history whose singleness of purpose spurred them to great accomplishments. What factors in the life of each one combined to produce this singleness of purpose?

5. The role of wife and mother was considered the only valid one for a woman in the nineteenth century. Today there are many options open to women—to be married or single; to be a wife, mother, homemaker, professional woman, or any combination of these. Does any one role have more validity than the others? Or do all have equal validity, depending upon individual choice? Explain your answer.

6. What models for today do you see in the life of Dorothea Dix?

# NOTES

## Chapter 1—Anne Hutchinson

[1] Helen Augur, *An American Jezebel: The Life of Anne Hutchinson* (New York: Brentano's, Inc., 1930), p. 272.

[2] *Ibid.,* pp. 17-18.

[3] Emery Battis, "Anne Hutchinson," in *Notable American Women, 1607–1950: A Biographical Dictionary,* vol. 2, ed. Edward T. James (Cambridge, Mass.: The Belknap Press, imprint of the Harvard University Press, 1971), pp. 245-246.

[4] *Ibid.,* p. 148.

[5] Marion L. Starkey, *The Congregational Way: The Role of the Pilgrims and Their Heirs in Shaping America* (New York: Doubleday & Company, Inc., 1966), p. 74.

[6] Battis, "Anne Hutchinson," *op. cit.,* p. 247.

[7] *Ibid.*

[8] Edmund S. Morgan, *The Puritan Dilemma: The Story of John Winthrop* (Boston: Little, Brown and Company, 1958), p. 134.

## Chapter 2—Abigail Adams

[1] L. H. Butterfield, "Abigail Smith Adams," in *Notable American Women, 1607–1950: A Biographical Dictionary,* vol. 1, ed. Edward T. James (Cambridge, Mass.: The Belknap Press, imprint of Harvard University Press, 1971), p. 6. First published in *Adams Family Correspondence,* vol. 1 and 2, ed. L. H. Butterfield (Cambridge, Mass.: The Belknap Press of Harvard University Press, 1963). © 1963 by Massachusetts Historical Society.

[2] *The Book of Abigail and John: Selected Letters of the Adams Family, 1762–1784,* ed. L. H. Butterfield, Marc Friedlaender, and Mary-Jo Kline (Cambridge, Mass.: Harvard University Press, 1975), p. 24. First published in *Adams Family Correspondence*, vol. 1 and 2, ed. L. H. Butterfield (Cambridge, Mass.: The Belknap Press of Harvard University Press, 1963). © 1963 by Massachusetts Historical Society.

[3] *Ibid.*, p. 25.

[4] *Ibid*, p. 48.

[5] *Ibid.*, p. 59.

[6] *Ibid.*, p. 121.

[7] *Ibid.*, pp. 122-123.

[8] L. H. Butterfield, "Abigail Smith Adams," *op. cit.*, p. 7.

[9] *The Book of Abigail and John: Selected Letters of the Adams Family, 1762–1784*, p. 130.

[10] *Ibid.*, p. 90.

[11] *Ibid.*, p. 108.

[12] *Ibid.*, p. 182.

[13] *Ibid.*, p. 184.

[14] *Familiar Letters of John Adams and His Wife, Abigail Adams, During the Revolution*, with a memoir of Mrs. Adams by Charles Francis Adams (Plainview, N.Y.: Books for Libraries Press, Inc., first published in 1875, reprinted, 1970). p. xxvi.

[15] *The Founding Fathers. John Adams: A Biography in His Own Words,* ed. James Bishop Peabody (New York: Newsweek Books, distributed by Harper & Row, Publishers, Inc., 1973), p. 399. First published in Josiah Quincy, *Figures of the Past* (Boston: Little, Brown and Company, 1926).

[16] *Familiar Letters of John Adams and His Wife, Abigail Adams, During the Revolution*, p. xxix.

[17] John Murray Allison, *Adams and Jefferson: The Story of a Friendship* (Norman, Okla.: University of Oklahoma Press, 1966), p. 281.

[18] *The Founding Fathers: John Adams, A Biography in His Own Words*, p. 404.

[19] *New Letters of Abigail Adams, 1788-1801*, ed. Stewart Mitchell (Boston: Houghton Mifflin Company, 1947), pp. 211-212.

## Chapter 3—The Grimké Sisters

[1] Catherine H. Birney, *The Grimké Sisters: Sarah and Angelina Grimké, The First American Women Advocates of Abolition and Women's Rights* (Boston: Lee and Shepard Publishers, 1885; republished St. Clair Shores, Mich.: Scholarly Press, Inc., 1970), p. 12.

[2] Angelina Emily Grimké, *Appeal to the Christian Women of the South* (New York: Arno Press, Inc., and The New York Times, 1969), pp. 1-18.

[3] *Ibid.*, p. 25.

[4] Gerda Lerner, *The Grimké Sisters from South Carolina: Rebels Against Slavery* (Boston: Houghton Mifflin Company, 1967), p. 94.

[5] *Ibid.*, p. 145.

[6] *Ibid.*, p. 166.

[7] Betty L. Fladeland, "Sarah Moore and Angelina Emily Grimké," in *Notable American Women, 1607-1950: A Biographical Dictionary*, vol. 2, ed. Edward T. James (Cambridge, Mass.: The Belknap Press, imprint of Harvard University Press, 1971), p. 98.

[8] Sarah M. Grimké, *Letters on the Equality of the Sexes and the Condition of Women Addressed to Mary S. Parker, President of the Boston Female Anti-Slavery Society* (New York: Burt Franklin & Company, Inc., first published, 1838; reprinted 1970), p. 10.

## Chapter 4—Sojourner Truth

[1] Jacqueline Bernard, *Journey Toward Freedom: The Story of Sojourner Truth* (New York: W. W. Norton & Company, Inc., 1967), pp. 119-122. Reprinted by permission of the author.

[2] Saunders Redding, "Sojourner Truth," in *Notable American Women, 1607-1950: A Biographical Dictionary*, vol. 3, ed. Edward T. James (Cambridge, Mass.: The Belknap Press, imprint of the Harvard University Press, 1971), p. 480.

[3] Hertha Pauli, *Her Name Was Sojourner Truth* (New York: Appleton-Century-Crofts, 1962), p. 174. Copyright © 1962 by Hertha Pauli.

[4] Bernard, *op. cit.*, pp. 166-167.

[5] *The American Negro—His Story and Literature: Narrative of Sojourner Truth and Book of Life* (first published, Battle Creek, Mich., for the author, 1878; reprinted New York: Arno Press, Inc., and The New York Times, 1968), p. 312.

[6] Arthur Huff Fauset, *Sojourner Truth: God's Faithful Pilgrim* (Chapel Hill: University of North Carolina Press, 1944), p. 140.

[7] Bernard, *op. cit.*, p. 209.

[8] *Ibid.*, pp. 251-252.

[9] Redding, "Sojourner Truth," *op. cit.*, p. 481.

[10] Bernard, *op. cit.*, p. 253.

[11] *Ibid.*, p. 107.

## Chapter 5—Dorothea Dix

[1] Helen E. Marshall, *Dorothea Dix: Forgotten Samaritan* (New York: Russell & Russell, Publishers, 1967), p. 17.

[2] *Ibid.*, pp. 34-40.

[3] "Memorial to the Legislature of Massachusetts, 1843," Dorothea Dix, *On Behalf of the Insane Poor* in *Poverty, U.S.A.: The Historical Record*, ed. David J. Rothman (New York: Arno Press, Inc., and The New York Times, 1971), p. 9. Reprinted by Arno Press, Inc., 1971.

[4] *Ibid.*, p. 4.

[5] Francis Tiffany, *Life of Dorothea Lynde Dix* (New York: Houghton Mifflin Company, 1891), p. 375.